WITHDRAWN

St. Louis Community
College

The Left-Handed Designer

Seymour Chwast

The Left-Handed Designer

Edited by Steven Heller

Harry N. Abrams, Inc., Publishers, New York

This book is dedicated
to the memory of my father,
Aaron L. Chwast

Many friends and colleagues have been involved in my work with encouragement and collaboration for whom I express my deep appreciation. Some of them are listed here:

PUSH PIN EDITIONS
Designer: Seymour Chwast
Assistant Designer: Doris Neulinger
Production: Caroline Ginesi
Assistant Editors: Judy Palaferro, Debora Schuler

Library of Congress Cataloging in Publication Data

Chwast, Seymour.
The left-handed designer.

Bibliography: p.
1. Chwast, Seymour. 2. Graphic arts—Technique.
I. Title.
NC999.4.C48A4 1985 741.6′092′4 85–3922
ISBN 0–8109–1284–9

Published in 1985 by Harry N. Abrams, Incorporated, New York

Printed and bound in Japan

Acknowledgments

Phyllis Flood
Ilse Lebrecht
Evelyne Menasce
Milton Glaser
Malcolm Forbes
Sandra Ruch
Alan Peckolick
George Leavitt
Edward Sorel
Lilly Filipow
Esther Newman
Michael Aron
Walter Bernard
Vincent Ceci
Reynold Ruffins
Haruo Miyauchi
Murry Gelberg
Ken Robbins
Harris Lewine
Jane Lander
Paula Scher
Richard Mantel
Martin Moskof
R.O. Blechman
James McMullan
Pamela Vassil
Rudy Hoglund
Ruth Ansel
Kevin Gatta
Juan Tenorio
Cleveland Dobson
Gail Stampar
Ronald Smith James
Bob Morton
Samuel N. Antupit
Edward Booth-Clibborn

Contents

Steven Heller Interviews Seymour Chwast

Has your left-handedness influenced your work in any way? I've always been left-handed. Although my mother would deny it, she tried to get me to use my right hand more often, because it was considered a handicap—and evidence of my being a little odd. However, being odd gave me a terrific excuse for being an artist.

Originally I thought I was going to go to work in animation, because my mother overheard some people on the subway say that a person could make $35 a week working for Walt Disney. Needless to say, I was very interested in cartooning when I was five or six.

How long did your Disney aspirations last? Until I was sixteen, when I entered Abraham Lincoln High School in Brooklyn. The art class was taught by Leon Friend, a charismatic father figure who gave me an appreciation of typography and graphic design, and equated success in these areas with achieving nirvana. Friend introduced us to the great poster designers and to the work of some of his own students who had become accomplished themselves.

It's remarkable that a New York City public high school was so richly endowed. With this knowledge of typography and design, what did you do when you graduated? I went to Cooper Union, an art and architecture college in New York City. I owe my life and career to that experience. Sidney Delevante, my drawing teacher, revolutionized my way of thinking by making me start everything from zero with nothing preconceived. I also learned from him that, while my work had a point of view, there were infinite ways of expressing it. He helped me find ways that were consistent with my personality. I learned as much from some of my fellow students as I did from the teachers. Milton Glaser, Ed Sorel, and Reynold Ruffins were in my class. I also learned by looking at paintings by artists such as Rouault and Klee. Most importantly, at that time there was an exhibition of work by Ben Shahn at the Museum of Modern Art that proved to be a major influence. The power of his work emerged from the immediacy and directness of his style. It was awkward and decorative, like the work of the primitive artists, but the depth of his feeling and his humanity were always there.

I also took painting courses, but my paintings turned out to be cartoons. My first woodcut and my one and only lithograph in printmaking class were both funny. I was very serious about what I was doing, but I knew that my work was different from that of most of the other students who always seemed to be painting onion shapes.

You once told me that Goya and Daumier affected your work. How did you use them? Theirs was a passion motivated by their beliefs about politics and society. Their work had bite. They expressed *feeling* you could only get through a print, and that approach conformed to the way I was thinking in those days. I was active politically, and I was sympathetic to radical and pacifist causes.

I could only be good as a nonconformist. Art has to establish its own order and authority, while attacking the existing one. I have tried to use my assignments as platforms for whatever I have to say, while the client, in turn, uses me. When Push Pin Studios had its exhibition at the Louvre, critics were surprised to see such eccentric and subversive work coming from corporate America.

You spoke about nonconformity. Whom or what were you rebelling against? In about 1950, we were coming to the end of the era of the glorious illustrator—the people who worked for the *Saturday Evening Post* and various women's magazines. Norman Rockwell and the realistic illustrators were the enemy, because their work was sentimental. Their storytelling renderings seemed pedestrian compared to the work of George Grosz and Saul Steinberg. We responded to a rise of interest in our interior psyches rather than our exterior surroundings. I was also concerned with the process of reproduction—how the type looked, how the spread looked, how the work was being used. Design was much more important to me than the illustration alone.

So, after leaving college you decided to wed the two forms? I worked for George Kirkorian at the *New York Times* promotion department as a junior designer. I was able to create my own designs and illustrations, which included woodcuts—rather innovative for that time. I left to work for *Esquire,* my first job failure in a string of failures that included jobs at a design studio and an advertising agency. Herb Lubalin fired me at Sudler and Hennessey because I couldn't do comprehensive sketches. I worked for the *House & Garden* and *Glamour* promotion departments for about a year, and about that time Ed Sorel, Reynold Ruffins, and I developed something called *The Push Pin Almanack,* which we mailed out as a bi-monthly personal promotion piece. Indeed, it resulted in a great many freelance assignments.

The almanac was a convenient vehicle. While it had its own conventions, we were able to apply our own typographic ideas, and do quaint drawings, consistent not only with almanacs, but with the style of the times. Each issue, which we edited and designed, was based on a different theme.

Then, with Milton and Ed, Push Pin Studios was founded. In those low-tech days of 1954 it took very little capital to go into business. We used the name Push Pin Studios because the *Almanack* was helping us to gain a reputation. A couple of film strips kept us busy until other assignments started coming in.

Did each of you have an individual style? Was style important to you then? Yes. Ed worked with flat shapes which he had learned at Cooper, completely different from the way he works now. Milton used a fine pen, resulting in beautiful engraving-style drawings. All in the spirit of decorative illustration. I made woodcuts, monoprints, and drawings with a Speedball pen, which gave me a bold line.

Cutting a block is a physical act. While the work is in the cutting, magic occurs as the image emerges from the wood. Some discipline is needed in the cutting, since the areas that are carved out are the ones that will *not* print. Another method I used—and still use—involved colored pencils and acrylics on chipboard. The chipboard material is in a middle gray and has a hard surface. Magic also occurs when the image emerges as I apply my light and dark colors.

It sounds like you were bringing techniques to illustration that were not familiar. It seems to me that illustration in America, then, was mostly painting and a little drawing. Through the *Push Pin Graphic,* which succeeded the *Almanack,* we were doing illustration that technically and stylistically wasn't being done. Also, our typographic style, which was based on traditional approaches, was unique to that period.

Push Pin, for the first time, looked back at the tradition of graphics and modernized it. Would you say that it was a significant contribution to the field? Well, I had no idea that Push Pin was going to be as influential as it was. I had no overview of how the studio work was evolving or what we were contributing to the field of graphic design. I was just doing jobs and allowing everything—old posters, rubber stamps, antiques, modern paintings—to influence my work. Surrealism also affected me: misplaced objects; the idea of doing fairly realistic situations that are confounded by odd relationships and strangely connected elements. In the early sixties I was also developing an approach based on primitive and folk art. However, I found that around 1950 designers had come to the end of a period of evolving style. We came to that point because extensive publishing allowed us to observe and digest everything that had been done before. We started borrowing from the past. First we were interested in Victoriana, which had a vigor, a charm and directness derived from the limitations of the printing methods of the period. Then we discovered Art Nouveau and Art Deco. Psychedelia was somewhat original, but it had Jugendstil roots. New Wave was a recycling of Constructivism with variations. If any truly original styles have been developed in the last three decades, more time will be needed to provide perspective on them.

Style in general, is useful because it provides immediate clues to the message. It might signal "elegance" or "modernity," for instance. Putting an old style in a new context is surprising, because certain relationships may be ironic; others may fit perfectly well. But they allow a designer to make very graphic statements.

As you were introduced to different approaches, they became part of your own style. Yes, and I was able to do it freely in the *Push Pin Graphic.*

There's an interesting thing happening here. Commercial art means that you're working for commerce, which means that you have a client you must answer to; someone who has to approve of what you're doing. The *Graphic* was a way of doing something without anybody's approval but your own. The art directors responded to that. They might not have been able to sell our approach to their clients, but selling it to *them* was half the battle. It proved that we could think, organize, and translate literary material into visual statements. But also, I think our work has always been accessible. It used to be called "far out" in those days, but if our interpretation was right the style was unimportant to the client. More importantly we were *inventing* things. It's great when a discovery is made and applied to something previously commonplace. One such seemingly unimportant breakthrough was when Milton and I, in the *Push Pin Graphic,* put our drawings in boxes with rounded corners: a few months later we noticed rounded corners appearing elsewhere by other designers. That lasted as a motif for a few years. Another was when I did my first drawing with a broken line. Other broken-line artists popped up almost immediately.

You have so many styles. Did you change your approach as much to get away from imitators as to grow? Growth comes out of our creative curiosity to explore and invent. On a banal level it also satisfies our need to compete with our peers and keep one step ahead of our imitators. Drawing and concept cannot be imitated but style *can.* When that occurs vitality is soon gone.

Are you a designer who illustrates or an illustrator who designs? I am a designer who illustrates. I observe the formal principles of design (proportion, harmony, dynamics, symmetry, line, mass, texture) while I am manipulating elements to suit my purposes. The way I articulate the solution is most often with an illustration (which is most often the client's expectation).

How do you approach your drawing? I often battle with the paper. While I could never work with a crow quill, a Speedball pen or Rapidograph enables me to bear down on the paper.

My drawing is weak. But I am not as interested in that as I am in making a graphic idea work. That's why I'm less concerned with *finish.* The concept has always been most important, and therefore I look for the style most appropriate to express the idea. Surface, neatness, rendering, and craft are things that interest me less.

With typography, are you more conservative than with illustration? I play with type since it is a design element, but I respect its rules. The rules of drawing and basic design are also supreme, but they can be stretched and expanded. Choice of type style is an esthetic judgment. Observing an exquisite type face beautifully displayed is a sublime experience. But what we have is the widest range of ugly faces and a willingness on the part of designers to use them. I have a fantasy in which I become Type Czar of the World and eradicate all the bad ones.

My sense of typography is rooted in tradition, so it tends to be conservative. For instance, typographic letter forms were originally designed to fit the limitations of the metal. I disavow ligatures and tend to print my type in black. Understanding the rules means knowing what you can't do. I generally don't illustrate with typography, but rather use it to integrate with, or counterbalance the image. That's why I don't use freehand lettering, which competes with the image. Sometimes my type may be elegant to go along with a very inelegant drawing.

How far do you go to serve your clients? The client's message must be presented in the most clear and accessible manner possible. As long as I take care of the client's needs I can be as outrageous or as unexpected as I want. However, my reputation doesn't matter if I don't communicate the message, or if the client has no understanding of what I'm trying to do. After all, my graphic idea and the client's story have to be harmonious.

Do you struggle coming up with ideas? You have to know how far to go. If the idea doesn't gel after a certain amount of struggle you have to give up. I read once about the concepts of the lateral idea and the vertical idea. If you dig a hole and it's in the wrong place, digging it deeper isn't going to help. The lateral idea is when you skip over and dig someplace else.

Sometimes I get ideas in bed just after the alarm goes off. Other times I use references. Occasionally a photograph or an old poster may spark off a notion. If I'm parodying a style of the past, I will use all the source material necessary to replicate the gestalt of the style.

Do you ever get to a point of frustration, or fear, that what you are doing is tired? Is there ever the compulsion to do something different for the sake of doing it? It's a prize fight. The creative urge versus constraints—either of time, or the client, or my own laziness or lack of patience. However, I'm always working on half a dozen things simultaneously, in different stages. It's the way I've trained myself. Actually, I need deadlines. What's worse is being down to the last job, because what motivates me is very often getting on to the next thing. While I'm working on drawings I might be, at the same time, conceptualizing and designing in collaboration with my partner, Alan Peckolick, or other members of my studio.

Not only are you an illustrator and a designer, but you also are an art director. Is it difficult to function in that capacity? As art director I might have to give an assignment to an illustrator, based on an idea, either vaguely formed or something very specific. That's difficult for me, because as an illustrator I have my own sensibilities, and I have to project myself into what is good for the illustrator as well as what is good for the project. I try to allow the illustrator the same freedom I would want for myself.

Do you have taboos? Are there jobs that you won't touch? Are there techniques that you won't use? I wouldn't work for a politician whose philosophy is radically different from mine. And I wouldn't work for the armed forces of any country. Sometimes I take a cigarette assignment and sometimes I don't. It's difficult for me to inject my own biases in deciding when not to take an assignment because as the principal of a studio, people depend on me to make a living.

Watercolor and delicate pen work require craftsmanship and drawing ability I do not have. I haven't done an airbrush illustration since I lost a poster contest in high school. However, there are aspects in all styles that I can respond to, although I might not have the skill or interest to try them. Furthermore, there isn't a color I wouldn't use, except chartreuse.

How would you characterize your use of wit? Is it a vehicle or a weapon? I attempt satire or wit most of the time because I see so much in the human condition that can be ridiculed. Is it a vehicle or a a weapon? Wit needs no reason.

Do you keep sketches or a notebook of ideas? I make a lot of preparation sketches but I throw them away as soon as the job is complete. It's part of my craving for order. Generally, unless it's a poster, I work full size, and about four minutes into the assignment, when I realize I'll never draw again, I start making thumbnails, and generally an idea forms. Then it becomes necessary for me to go back to full size again and hope that I can keep some of the energy that was in the thumbnail. As soon as I have finished drawing, I get rid of all my sketches as quickly as possible.

Wait a minute. You said "you'll never draw again." Are you serious? It happens with every job. With the *last* drawing, I've had my *last* good idea. It's a struggle, since everything's been done. I imagine for the younger generation it's going to be harder. They have to invent something completely different.

Do children's books allow you more freedom than adult illustration? Children respond to the kind of artwork I do. What's odd is that my children's illustrations are sometimes considered too sophisticated. I don't understand that at all, unless my work is not cute enough for children. Ironically, those reactions go against my innocent, head-on style. You see, there's nothing behind what I'm doing. It's all laid out. There's no symbolism, no mystery.

Do you still feel you're communicating a point of view? What I do *is* my point of view. It pleases me that there is a bond with others that occurs when this happens.

And do you feel that doing commercial art does that more effectively than other art forms? I love working with media, working with printing papers, finding new methods of printing. I am still amazed and get great satisfaction in seeing a drawing that I had done the day before printed in the *New York Times*. My work as a commercial artist, seen by millions, gives me joy and satisfaction that "fine" art cannot supply. Besides, since the sixties there have been so many crossovers in artists and the way artists work that the line between fine and applied art has become blurred. The only real difference between them is the intent.

You never had the desire to do art for art's sake? Oh, no. I found that I needed a message or literary reference to react to. Solving esthetic problems was either beyond me, or seemed self-indulgent, considering my working-class background.

What is different with your work today, vis-a-vis the past? What have you learned? What would you still like to accomplish? What I had in the past that I no longer have is innocence. I've been to too many shows, and seen too many annuals. I've exchanged that innocence for professionalism. I would like to have both.

Ultimately, my personal goal is to gain control so that I can carry out my ideas. With enough clout, and with the help of my partners, Alan Peckolick and Phyllis Flood, I can convince the client that my *unique* solution is the right one. In this manner I become a consultant rather than a mere supplier. That leverage allows me to resist compromise, giving me the freedom to follow my instincts, to build upon what I have done, and ultimately to create better graphic design.

One last question. You treat your right hand like a second child, and your left hand like royalty. Does your right hand serve any useful purpose? Well, yes. I use my right hand to hold my head up at the correct distance from my drawing table. I couldn't work any other way.

Biographical Notes

1931 Born in New York City
1948 Graduated from Abraham Lincoln High School, Brooklyn, N.Y.
1951 Graduated from the Cooper Union School of Art and Architecture
1954 Co-founded Push Pin Studios
1971 Elected to the Board of Directors, American Institute of Graphic Arts
1971–2 Co-designed and art directed *Audience* magazine
1975 Appointed member of Alliance Graphique Internationale
1975 Co-founded Push Pin Press
1976 Editor and publisher of the Push Pin Graphic
1982 Director of Pushpin Lubalin Peckolick
1984 Inducted into the New York Art Directors Club Hall of Fame
1985 Director of The Pushpin Group

Museum and Gallery Solo and Group Exhibitions

United States

Mead Library Gallery, New York, 1969.
Brooklyn Museum, Brooklyn, New York, 1972.
University of Southern California, Fullerton, California, 1974.
Jorgensen Gallery, University of Connecticut, Storrs, Connecticut, 1977.
Kansas City Art Institute, Kansas City, Missouri, 1979.
Rochester Institute of Technology, Rochester, New York, 1980.
Atrium Gallery, University of Connecticut, Storrs, Connecticut, 1983.
Helander/Rubinstein Gallery, Palm Beach, Florida, 1983.
Schiller-Wapner Gallery, New York, 1984.
Arthur A. Houghton Gallery, The Cooper Union, New York, 1985.

Europe and Japan

Musée des Arts Décoratifs, Louvre, Paris, France, 1970.
Holland Festival in Leidestraat, the Netherlands, 1970.
Vienna-Amerika House, Vienna, Austria, 1970.
Musée des Arts Décoratifs, Lausanne, Switzerland, 1970.
Reed House, London, England, 1970.
Museum of Applied Arts, Belgrade, Yugoslavia, 1971.
Tokyu Department Store, Tokyo, Japan, 1973 and 1984.
Galerie Delpire, Paris, France, 1974 and 1980.
Chelsea School of Art, Chelsea Gallery, London, England, 1978.
Eighth International Poster Biennale, Warsaw, Poland, 1980.
Kunstgewerbemuseum, Zurich, Switzerland, 1981.
Fachberleich Gestaltung Darmstadt, Fine Arts Institute, Darmstadt, West Germany, 1981.
Gutenberg Museum, Mainz, West Germany, 1983.
Volkstheater am Park, Wiesbaden, West Germany, 1983.
Galerie Bartsch et Chariau, Munich, West Germany, 1984.
Centre Pompidou, Paris, France, 1985.

Bibliography

The work of Seymour Chwast has appeared in the following publications:

Graphis No. 62, Zurich, “The Push Pin Almanack,” 1955.
American Artist, New York, “Push Pin Studios,” September, 1958.
Graphis No. 80, Zurich, “The Push Pin Studios,” 1958.
Graphis No. 102, Zurich, “Seymour Chwast,” 1962.
Communication Arts, Palo Alto, CA, “The Push Pin Studios,” 1962.
Idea, Tokyo, “The Designers of the Push Pin Studios,” 1964.
Gebrauchsgrafik, Munich, “10 Jahre Push Pin Studios, New York,” 1964.
Design, London, “Revivalism Revisited,” 1968.
Newsweek, New York, “Design Gourmet,” February 10, 1968.
Publisher's Weekly, New York, “Louvre Holds Retrospective of Push Pin Studio's Graphics,” April 13, 1970.
Actuel, Paris, “Push Pin As It Likes It,” 1970.
The Push Pin Style, published by *Communication Arts,* Palo Alto, CA, 1970.
Creé, Paris, “Le Push Pin Studios,” 1970.
American Artist, New York, “Seymour Chwast: A Coney Island of the Head,” October, 1971.
The Push Pin Style of Design and Illustration, published by *Idea,* Tokyo, 1972.
Graphic Design, Tokyo, “Seymour Chwast and His Children's Books,” 1973.
Graphis No. 175, Zurich, “Seymour Chwast: 100 Heads,” 1974/75.
New York Times Magazine, New York, “Push Pin Conspiracy,” March 6, 1977.
Graphics Today, New York, “The Chwast Nobody Knows,” September, 1977.
Idea, Tokyo, “Important Graphic Designers of the Last Twenty-five Years,” 1978.
Graphis No. 197, Zurich, “A Studio Magazine Comes of Age,” 1978/79.
B à T, Paris, “Le Push Pin, vingt ans apres,” 1980.
Frankfurter Allgemeine Magazin, Frankfurt, “Mann Mit Nase, (Man With Nose): Seymour Chwast,” April, 1981.
The Book of Graphic Problem-Solving, by John Newcomb, R.R. Bowker, Ann Arbor, MI, “Seymour Chwast,” 1984.
Graphis No. 230, “Seymour Chwast Chairs,” Zurich, 1984.
USA 22, Washington, D.C., “A Push Pin Graphic,” n.d.

Collections

Seymour Chwast's works are in the permanent collections of:

Museum of Modern Art, New York
Gutenberg Museum, Mainz, West Germany
Israel Museum, Jerusalem
Library of Congress, Washington, D.C.
Cooper-Hewitt Museum of the Smithsonian Institution, New York
Stadtmuseum, Munich, West Germany

Books by Seymour Chwast

The Book of Battles, privately printed, 1957.
Connoisseur Book of the Cigar, designer, McGraw-Hill, 1967.
Sara's Granny & the Groodle, illustrator, Doubleday, 1967.
Still Another Number Book, designer, illustrator, McGraw-Hill, 1970.
Pancake King, designer and illustrator, Delacorte Press, 1970.
Mother Goose, designer and illustrator, Random House, 1971.
Still Another Children's Book, designer, illustrator, McGraw-Hill, 1972.
Limericks, designer and illustrator, Random House, 1972.
The Illustrated Cat, designer, Harmony Books, 1975.
Which One Is Different?, designer, Doubleday, 1975.
The Sweet Heart and Others, designer, Avon, 1975.
Sleepy Ida, illustrator, Pantheon Books, 1977.
The Literary Dog, designer, Berkeley Windhover, 1978.
Zabar's Deli Cook, designer and illustrator, Hawthorne Books, 1979.
Tall City, Wide Country, author, designer, and illustrator, Viking Press, 1983.
Art of New York, co-editor and designer, Harry N. Abrams, Inc., 1983.
Art Against War, co-editor and designer, Abbeville Press, 1984.
Happy Birthday Bach, designer and illustrator, Dolphin/Doubleday, 1985.

Credits

We have made every effort to correctly credit all the entries in this book. Please inform the publisher of any additions or corrections for future editions.

[1,3-5] Client: Mobil Oil
Art Director: Sandra Ruch

[2] Client: Mobil Oil
Art Director: Gordon Bowman

[6] Publication: *Rolling Stone*
Art Director: Chris Austopchuk

[7] Client: Museum of the Borough of Brooklyn
Director: Shelly Dinhoffer

[9] Client: Simpson Paper
Art Director: James Cross

[10] Client: Pushpin Lubalin Peckolick
Art Director: Seymour Chwast

[11] Client: Kansas City Art Institute
Designers: Seymour Chwast, Richard Mantel
Illustrator: Seymour Chwast

[12] Client: The Ink Tank
Director: R. O. Blechman

[13] Client: Peridot Films, Inc.
Art Director: Jordan Caldwell

[14] Client: Elektra Films, Inc.
Art Director: Sam Magdoff

[15] Publication: *New York* Magazine
Art Director: J. C. Suares

[16] Client: Poster Prints, Inc
Art Director: Unknown

[17] Client: Personality Posters
Art Director: Marty Geisler

[18] Client: June 12 Rally Committee
Art Director: Chad Dobson

[19] Client: Sony Corporation
Art Director: John W. Channell

[20] Client: Push Pin Studios
Art Director: Seymour Chwast

[21] Client: Galerie Bartsch et Chariau
Directors: Andre Bartsch, Joelle Chariau

[22] Client: Nouvelle Observateur
Director: Robert Delpire

[23] Client: Brooklyn Children's Museum
Directors: George W. Kelly, Gabrielle Pohle

[24] Client: Olivetti
Art Director: Giorgio Soavi
Designers: Seymour Chwast, Milton Glaser
Illustrator: Seymour Chwast

[25] Client: New York City Opera
Agency: Rumrill Hoyt
Art Director: Lila Sternglass

[26] Client: Art Institute of Fort Lauderdale
The Design Schools
Art Director: Ed Hamilton

[27] Client: Peugeot
Art Director: Robert Delpire

[28] Client: Tyler School of Art Print Workshop
Art Director: Warren Infield

[29] Client: Union Camp Paper
Agency: Henderson & Roll
Art Director: Hal Josephs

[30] Publication: *The New York Times Magazine*
Art Director: Ruth Ansel

[31] Publication: *The New York Times*
Art Director: J. C. Suares

[32] Client: Push Pin Productions, Inc.
Director: Phyllis Flood
Art Director/Designer: Seymour Chwast
Illustrators: Seymour Chwast, Richard Mantel
Haruo Miyauchi, Peter Ross

[33] Client: McDonald's System, Inc.
Art Director: Unknown

[34] Client: Associated Merchandising Corporation
Art Director: Doug Bertsch

[35] Client: Artone Ink
Art Director: Lou Strick

[36] Client: Meredith
Art Directors: Henri and Anny Chwast

[37] Client: Post Cereals
Agency: Young & Rubicam
Art Director: Unknown

[38] Client: Erlanger Beer
Agency: MCA Graham Advertising
Art Director: Norman Black
Designers: Seymour Chwast, Michael Aron
Illustrators: Laszlo Kubinyi, Michael Hostovich

[39] Client: Associated Merchandising Corporation
Art Director: Doug Bertsch
Production: Kevin Gatta
Illustrator: Eve Chwast

[40] Client: The Ink Tank
Director: R. O. Blechman

[41] Client: Lörke GmbH
Director: Gunther Lörke

[42] Publication: *Push Pin Graphic*
Illustrator: Haruo Miyauchi

[43] Client: Nickelodeon, Inc.
Art Director: Seymour Chwast

[44] Client: *Push Pin Almanack*
Push Pin Studios, Inc.
Designers: Seymour Chwast, Milton Glaser,
Reynold Ruffins

[45] Client: Biofitness Institute
Agency: Greenwood Consultants
Art Director: Kristin Joyce

[46] Publication: *Frankfurter Allgemeine Magazin*
Art Director: Hans-Georg Pospischil

[47] Publisher: McGraw-Hill, Inc.
Art Director: Harris Lewine

[48] Publisher: Avon Books
Editor: Peter Mayer
Illustrator: Robert Conrad, George Stavrinos, et al

[49] Publisher: American Showcase
Art Director: Seymour Chwast
Designers: Seymour Chwast, Richard Mantel, Michael Aron

[50] Publication: *Audience*
Art Directors: Seymour Chwast, Milton Glaser
Illustrator: Seymour Chwast
Photographers: Steve Myers, Ben Rose

[51] Publication: *Audience*
Art Directors: Seymour Chwast, Milton Glaser
Designer: Seymour Chwast

[52] Publication: *Rolling Stone*
Art Director: Chris Austopchuk
Illustrator: Seymour Chwast et al

[53] Publisher: Harry N. Abrams, Inc.
Art Director: Sam Antupit
Editors: Seymour Chwast, Steven Heller

[54] Publisher: Abbeville Press, Inc.
Editor: Walton Rawls

[55] Publisher: Crown Publishers, Inc.
Editors: Linda Sunshine, J. C. Suares

[56] Publisher: Doubleday & Co., Inc.
Editor: Jim Fitzgerald

[57] Publication: *The New York Times Magazine*
Art Director: Walter Bernard

[58] Publication: *The New York Times Magazine*
Art Director: Ruth Ansel

[59] Publication: *Time*
Art Director: Walter Bernard

[60,61] Publication: *The Atlantic*
Art Director: Judy Garlan

[62] Publication: *New York* Magazine
Art Directors: Walter Bernard, Milton Glaser

[63] Publication: *Idea*
Editor-in-Chief: Yoshihisa Ishihara

[64] Publication: *Graphis*
Editor: Walter Herdeg

[65] Client: NYC Department of Cultural Affairs
Agency: Grey Advertising
Art Director: Toshi

[66] Publisher: Holt, Rinehart & Winston
Art Director: Harris Lewine

[67] Publisher: Collier Books
Art Director: Margot Herr

[68] Publisher: Simon & Schuster, Inc.
Art Director: Frank Metz

[69] Publisher: Unknown
Art Director: Unknown

[70] Publication: *Idea*
Editor-in-Chief: Yoshihisa Ishihara

[71] Client: Roth-Handel
Agency: Euro Advertising
Art Director: Bernd Hanke

[72,73] Publication: *Graphis*
Editor: Walter Herdeg

[74] Publisher: Harcourt, Brace, Jovanovich, Inc.
Editor: Harris Lewine

[75] Publisher: Doubleday & Co., Inc.
Editor: Alex Gotfryd

[76] Publisher: Warner Paperback Library
Editor: Harris Lewine

[77,79] Publisher: Harper & Row Publishers, Inc.
Art Director: Bob Cheney

[78] Publisher: McGraw-Hill, Inc.
Editor: Harris Lewine

[80] Publisher: Harcourt, Brace, Jovanovich, Inc.
Editor: Harris Lewine

[81] Client: PCS
Art Director: Seymour Chwast

[82] Client: Toor Type
Art Director: Seymour Chwast

[83] Client: Pioneer-Moss
Art Director: Seymour Chwast

[84,86] Client: Metropolitan Printing Service
Art Director: Seymour Chwast

[87,93] Client: *Forbes*
Doremus & Co.
Art Director: John Garre

[88,89] Client: *Forbes*
Doremus & Co.
Art Director: Jeff Hoffman

[90,92] Client: *Forbes*
Doremus & Co.
Art Director: Paul Shields

[91,95] Client: *Forbes*
Doremus & Co.
Art Director: Vinnie Longo

[94] Client: *Forbes*
Doremus & Co.
Art Director: Fred Yantz

[96,98] Publication: *Frankfurter Allgemeine Magazin*
Art Director: Hans-Georg Pospischil

[99] Publication: *Evergreen Review*
Art Director: Ken Deardoff

[100] Client/Designer: Mo Lebowitz
Illustrator: Seymour Chwast

[101] Publication: *Audience*
Art Directors: Seymour Chwast, Milton Glaser

[102] Publication: *The Atlantic*
Art Director: Judy Garlan

[103] Publication: *The New York Times*
Art Director: J. C. Suares

[104] Publication: *The Atlantic*
Art Director: Adrian Taylor

[105] Publication: *The New York Times Magazine*
Art Director: Ruth Ansel

[106,107] Publication: *The New York Times*, Op-Ed Page
Art Director: J. C. Suares

[108] Publication: *The New York Times*
Art Director: Jerelle Kraus

[109,110] Publication: *Frankfurter Allgemeine Magazin*
Art Director: Willy Fleckhaus

[111] Client: Brook Hollow Hilton/Anchorage Restaurant
Agency: Metzdorf Advertising
Art Director: Sherri Oldham

[112] Publication: *The New York Times Magazine*
Art Director: Ruth Ansel

[113] Publication: *The Boston Globe*
Art Director: Ronn Campisi

[114] Client: Greengrass Gallery
Director: Seymour Chwast

[116] Publication: *Frankfurter Allgemeine Magazin*
Art Directors: Willy Fleckhaus, Hans-Georg Pospischil

[117] Client: Mead Library of Ideas
Art Director: Joseph Massina

[118] Publication: *Esquire*
Art Director: Marjory Peters

[119] Publication: *Audience*
Art Directors: Seymour Chwast, Milton Glaser
Illustrator: Seymour Chwast

[120] Client: Gebr. Schmidt Druckfarben
Art Director: Olaf Leu

[121] Client: CBS Records
Art Director: Eloise Vega

[122,125,128] Client: CBS Records
Art Director: Paula Scher

[126] Client: CBS Records
Art Director: Henrietta Condak

[127] Client: Atlantic Records
Art Directors: Abie Sussman, Bob Defrin

[129] Publisher: Delacorte Press
Designer: Seymour Chwast

[130,131] Publisher: Random House, Inc.
Art Director: Jerry Harrison

[132] Publisher: Viking Penguin Inc.
Editor: Deborah Brody

[133] Publisher: Editions Tournesol
Editors: Etienne Delessert, Rita Marshall

[134,136] Publisher: McGraw-Hill, Inc.
Author: Seymour Chwast, Martin Moskof
Editor: Eleanor Nichols

[137,139] Publication: *Push Pin Graphic*
Art Director: Seymour Chwast

[140] Publication: *Push Pin Graphic*
Art Directors: Seymour Chwast, Milton Glaser

[141-150] Publication: *Push Pin Graphic*
Art Director: Seymour Chwast

[151] Client: The Ink Tank
Producer: The Ink Tank
Director: R. O. Blechman
Animators: Ed Smith, Tissa David

[154] Publication: *Push Pin Graphic*
Art Director: Seymour Chwast

[155] Publisher: Doubleday & Co., Inc.
Editor: Jim Fitzgerald

[156-58,160] Printmaker: Alexander Heinrici

The Process of Idea and Style: Nicholas Nickleby

British cartoon of 1821

Thomas Rowlandson print

Material Supplied:

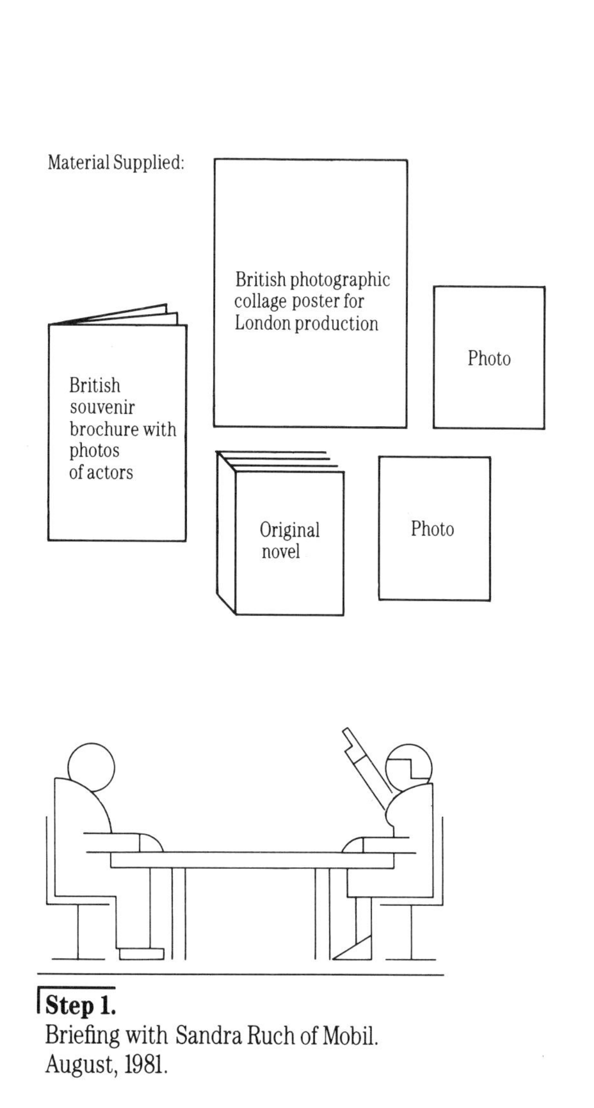

Step 1.
Briefing with Sandra Ruch of Mobil.
August, 1981.

Step 2.
Research.

"I like it... but change Kate and Smike."

Step 3.
Development and presentation of first sketch.

Nicholas Nickleby was playing in London when I was first presented with this poster assignment by Sandra Ruch of Mobil. I usually have a videotape to view when I do a job for a Mobil presentation, but in this case I was given the book and a press kit with stills from the British stage production.

I needed a device with which I could showcase some of the colorful Dickensian characters. The following diagram shows the way I solved this problem and adapted the concept in various media. The idea came from an 1821 British political cartoon, which showed a ladder with people perched on it. My first version, with a full-length Nicholas under the ladder, was printed as a teaser ad in newspapers a few months before the telecast. Once in print, I realized that the drawing had no scale or contrast. Luckily, I still had time to change the poster with an obvious solution: the ladder would rest on the shoulders of a greatly enlarged Nicholas.

By the time the production was aired, most of America was familiar with the image. It was inevitable that we animate it as the introduction to the telecast.

Revised sketch

Finished art for black-and-white ad

Finished art with gray tones

Proof

Changed head

Step 4.
Preparation of announcement ad months preceding air-date.

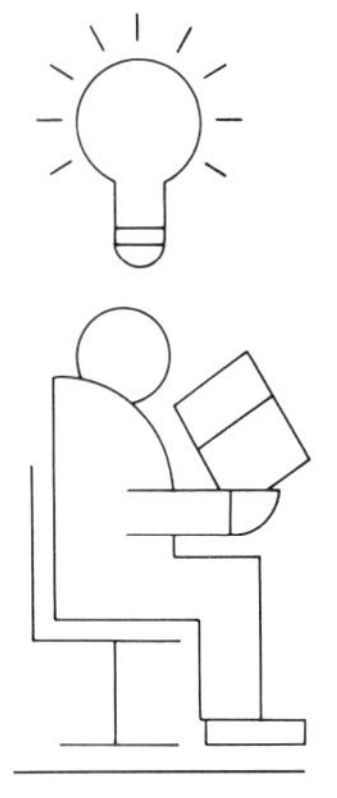

Step 5.
Revelation. I realized that the image would improve if the ladder were on Nicholas's shoulder.

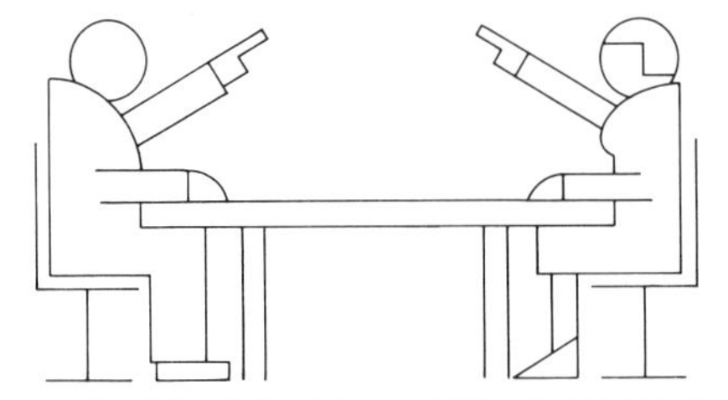

Step 6.
Presentation of revised prototype ad for poster and other applications.

Record jacket for MGM/UA

Penguin Book cover

Revised art in outline

I fill in the outline with Cello-Tak colors as a guide to the printer who matches those colors to make his color separations.

Mechanical

Completed poster

Step 7.
Development of collateral materials and products.

Step 8.
Preparation of a limited edition poster.

Step 9.
Supervision of printing at Crafton Graphics.

Accepted storyboard designed with R.O. Blechman and produced by Ink Tank

Storyboard provides idea for ad

Full page newspaper ad

Full page newspaper ad

Herbert Schmertz of Mobil suggests additional poster based on lettering for storyboard

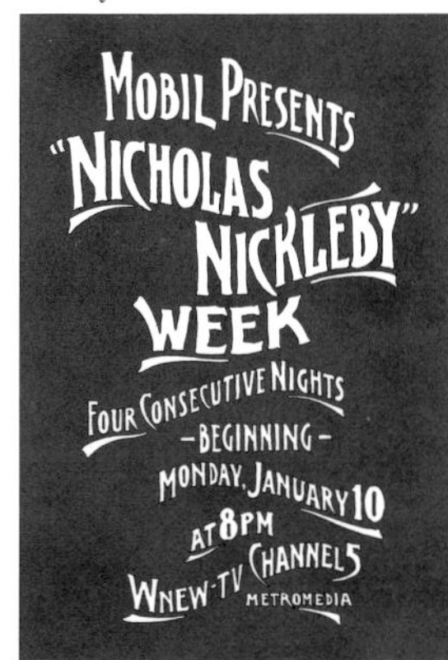

Single page magazine ad

Small space newspaper ad

Sandra Ruch conceives the idea of using characters from the animated titles in a double page newspaper ad.

Character sketches for animation

Step 10.
Design of animated on-air titles and promos.

Step 11.
Preparation of print advertising.

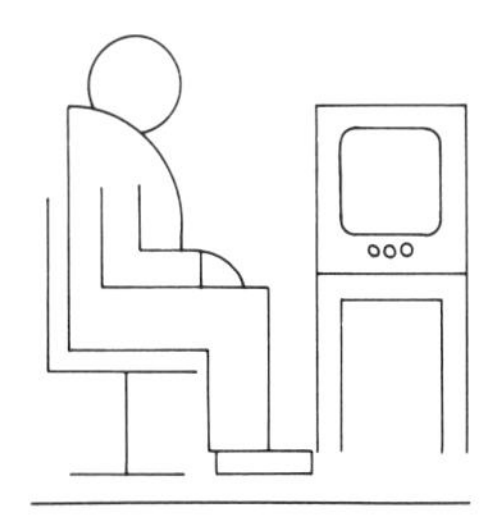

Step 12.
Watching *Nicholas Nickleby* telecast.
January, 1983.

Graphic Design

The poster—with its scale, visibility, immediacy, and its afterlife as "art"—offers compelling possibilities. [1] Poster for a Mobil Showcase Network presentation of Dickens's *Nicholas Nickleby.*

1

[2] Doug Henning is a magician in the Houdini tradition. This poster for Mobil was designed to approximate a Victorian magic poster common in Harry Houdini's time.

[3] Most of the time I come up with the ideas for the Mobil posters. For *I Claudius* I wasn't able to come up with anything better than the image used for the TV program titles, filmed in live action, in which a snake crawls over a mosaic tiled floor. I rendered Claudius as a mosaic, and added the goblet with the wine/blood spilling out, lending drama to the composition. The lettering chosen is closer to the style used in some New York subway stations than to classical Roman letter forms, but it was necessary to add weight to the design. The real problem came on the technical side; I wanted to approximate the look of a nineteenth-century chromolithograph by using flat rather than process colors. I, therefore, didn't supply the printer with a painting; instead I prepared a black outline and a color guide so that the printer could match the colors. Ordinarily this is not a difficult process, but here we needed fifteen colors plus a varnish. Each sheet passed through the press four times. On my part, it required four trips to the printer to supervise.

2

ALL ROME THOUGHT HIM A FOOL, BUT HIS GENIUS WAS SURVIVAL

I, CLAUDIUS

CHWAST

SUNDAYS AT 9 PM
ON CHANNEL 26 PBS

BEGINNING
NOVEMBER 6

MASTERPIECE
THEATRE

Mobil

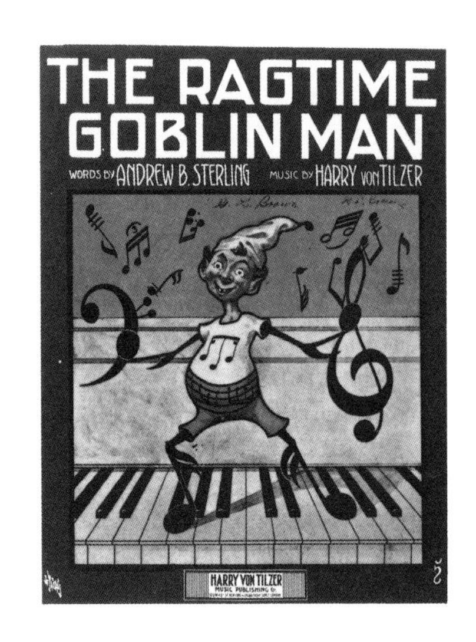
THE RAGTIME GOBLIN MAN
WORDS BY ANDREW B. STERLING
MUSIC BY HARRY VON TILZER
HARRY VON TILZER

SONG BY SONG
BY ALAN JAY LERNER: OCTOBER 22
ALMOST LIKE BEING IN LOVE
I COULD HAVE DANCED ALL NIGHT
ON A CLEAR DAY
CAMELOT
BY E.Y. HARBURG: NOVEMBER 26
OVER THE RAINBOW
IT'S ONLY A PAPER MOON
APRIL IN PARIS
HOW ARE THINGS IN GLOCCA MORRA
BY LORENZ HART: DECEMBER 31
WITH A SONG IN MY HEART
THIS CAN'T BE LOVE
MANHATTAN
BLUE MOON
BY DOROTHY FIELDS: JANUARY 28
I FEEL A SONG COMING ON
ON THE SUNNY SIDE OF THE STREET
I'M IN THE MOOD FOR LOVE
I CAN'T GIVE YOU ANYTHING BUT LOVE
BY HOWARD DIETZ: FEBRUARY 25
DANCING IN THE DARK
YOU AND THE NIGHT AND THE MUSIC
THAT'S ENTERTAINMENT
I LOVE LOUISA
BY OSCAR HAMMERSTEIN II: MARCH 24
OH WHAT A BEAUTIFUL MORNING
SOME ENCHANTED EVENING
IT MIGHT AS WELL BE SPRING
THE LAST TIME I SAW PARIS
BY SHELDON HARNICK: APRIL 28
IF I WERE A RICH MAN
WHAT MAKES ME LOVE HIM
SUNRISE, SUNSET
SHE LOVES ME
A MONTHLY MUSICAL SERIES
ON GREAT AMERICAN LYRICISTS
BEGINS OCTOBER 22
9 PM CHANNEL 13 PBS
HOST: NED SHERRIN
SEYMOUR CHWAST
Mobil

4

5

[4] *Song by Song* was inspired by a 1920s sheet music cover showing a gnome dancing on piano keys.

[5] For *Rumpole of the Bailey* I chose to portray the leading character in his dual roles as sleuth and lawyer. The Vishnu-like arms make the point.

[6] In this drawing of Graham Parker done for a review of his album in *Rolling Stone,* I took a page out of Peter Newell's topsy-turvy world. Once I saw Parker's symmetrical glasses in the photographic scrap I was given, I knew this would work.

[7] *Fun and Fantasy* was a poster announcing a show about leisure areas in Brooklyn, of which Coney Island is the most famous. The most recognizable image of Coney Island is the clown face trademark for George C. Tilyou's Steeplechase Park. I made the entire poster topsy-turvy.

[8] For a poster announcing an erotic film festival, I used a German decoupage mask and a simple outline to suggest the nature of the movies. The original was run on an offset press, but the version here, without type, was printed as a limited lithographic edition by Mourlot in Paris.

6

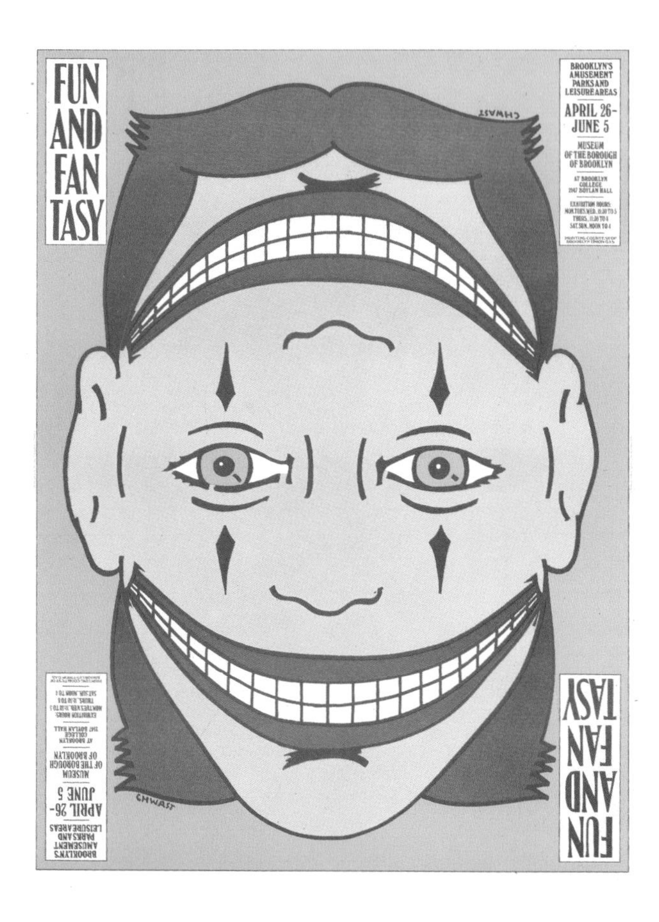

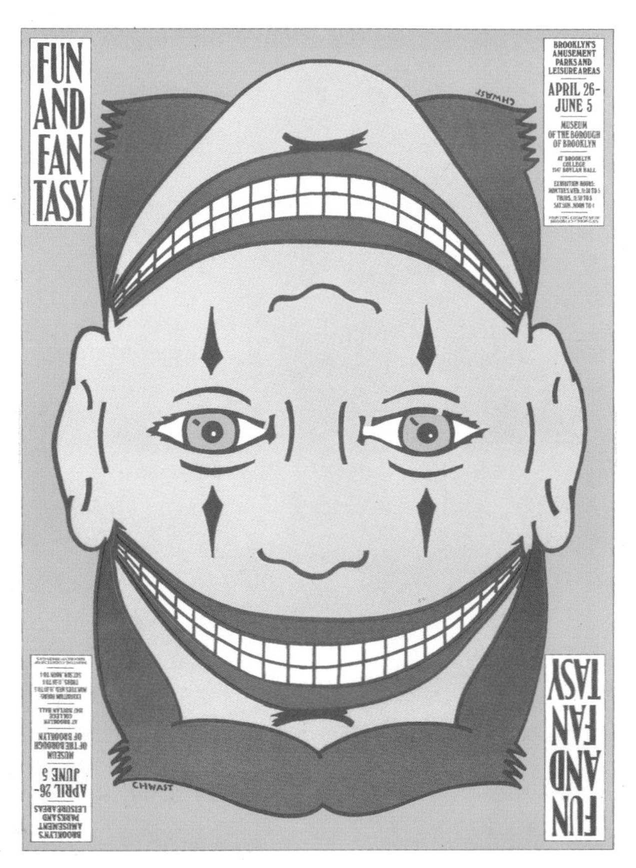

7

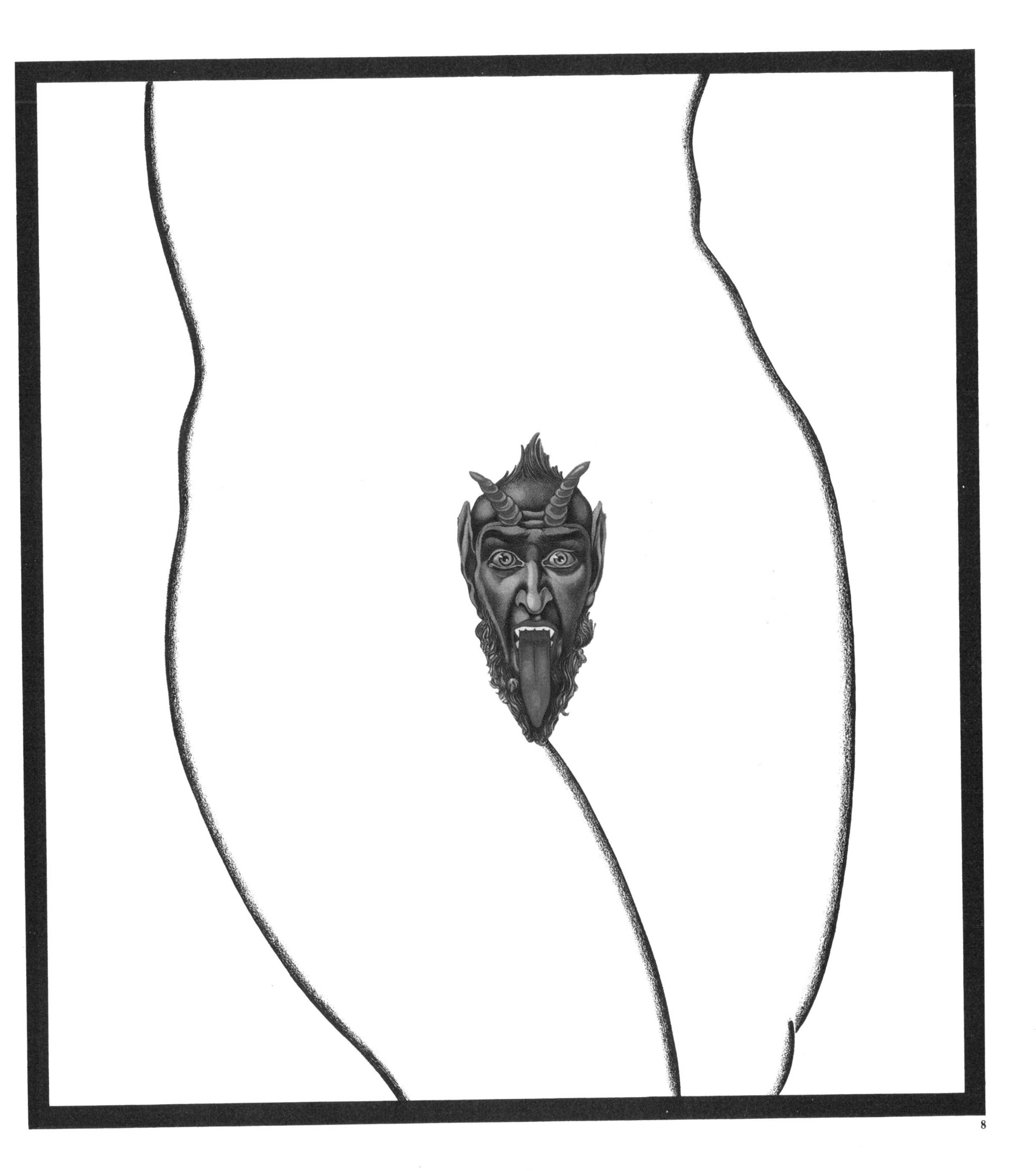

8

C O N N E C T I O N S

Seymour Chwast — "My work day is comprised of transforming ideas into visual expression through symbolism, manipulation, transformation, and exposition. Using these same methods I have tried to solve the problem of presenting an idealized portrait of those objects that are very important to me. They help prepare me for the day. I have integrated these ritualistic tools of washing and shaving because they have a common purpose, and that is to allow me to connect with the reality of my life."

SEYMOUR CHWAST

Simpson
making paper perform!

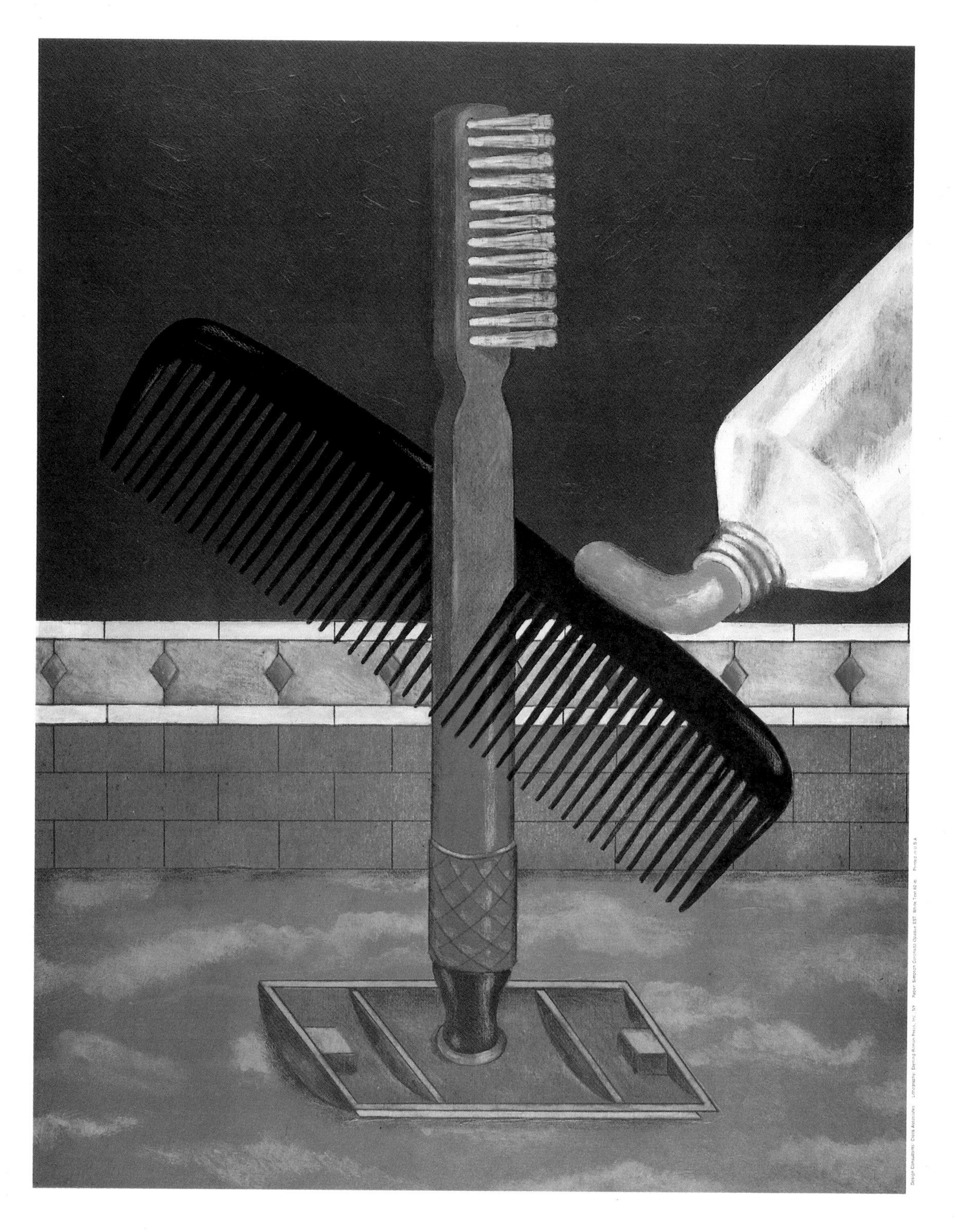

9

10

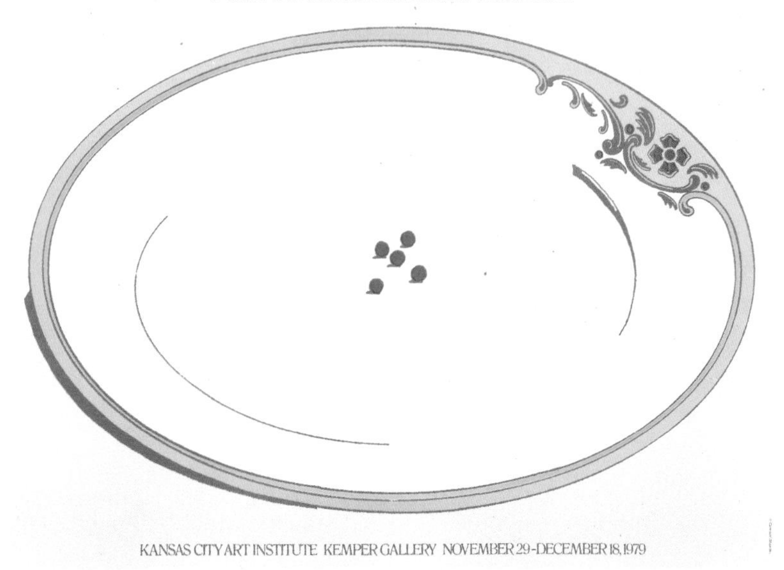

11

[9] *Connections* was one of a series of posters by various designers on the notion of connections of all kinds—emotional, physical, professional, even linguistic. I separated myself from the other graphic designers by using an illustrative approach and rendering the sundries that I connect with at the start of each day.

[10] *Carta Di Pasta* grew out of an Arcimboldo-inspired illustration for an article in *New York* Magazine. I used it again redrawn as a full page in the "Not Quite Human" issue of the *Push Pin Graphic*. Subsequently, I made it into a useful chart, embellished it with Art Deco lettering, and published it as a poster. One evening I was having dinner in an Italian restaurant. When I asked the waitress for the pasta of the day, she pointed to my poster, which was hanging over my head.

[11] *The Five Peas* was designed with Richard Mantel. The problem was to illustrate the contents of an expansive exhibition of Push Pin posters, prints, packaging, and publications for which there is no one symbolic image. The solution was based on the alliteration. The graphic strength of the poster comes from the tiny central image swimming in a sea of negative space.

[12] For the *Ink Tank* poster, I had to portray the characteristics of the eight very distinctive illustrators represented by R.O. Blechman's animation studio. Once I decided to take license with the human hand, I made patterns on the fingers that conformed to each artistic style. I made Blechman into the thumb because, as the boss, he opposes everybody.

[13] *Peridot* was a poster for a film animation studio. It represents the notion of creativity. The type is one of my deco alphabets, and the design of the dark figures was inspired by an image I saw fleetingly on an Italian olive oil can. The woman, or muse, on the couch emerges from an animation stand, while the skeptical clients leer at her.

[14] *Elektra* is a combination collage and drawing I made to express the idea of moving to new quarters. I love the serendipity achieved from pairing found graphic devices—it gives new life to something that originally had another function. Even the drawn elements are done in the style of the found ones. I particularly like the way the locomotive forms the "E."

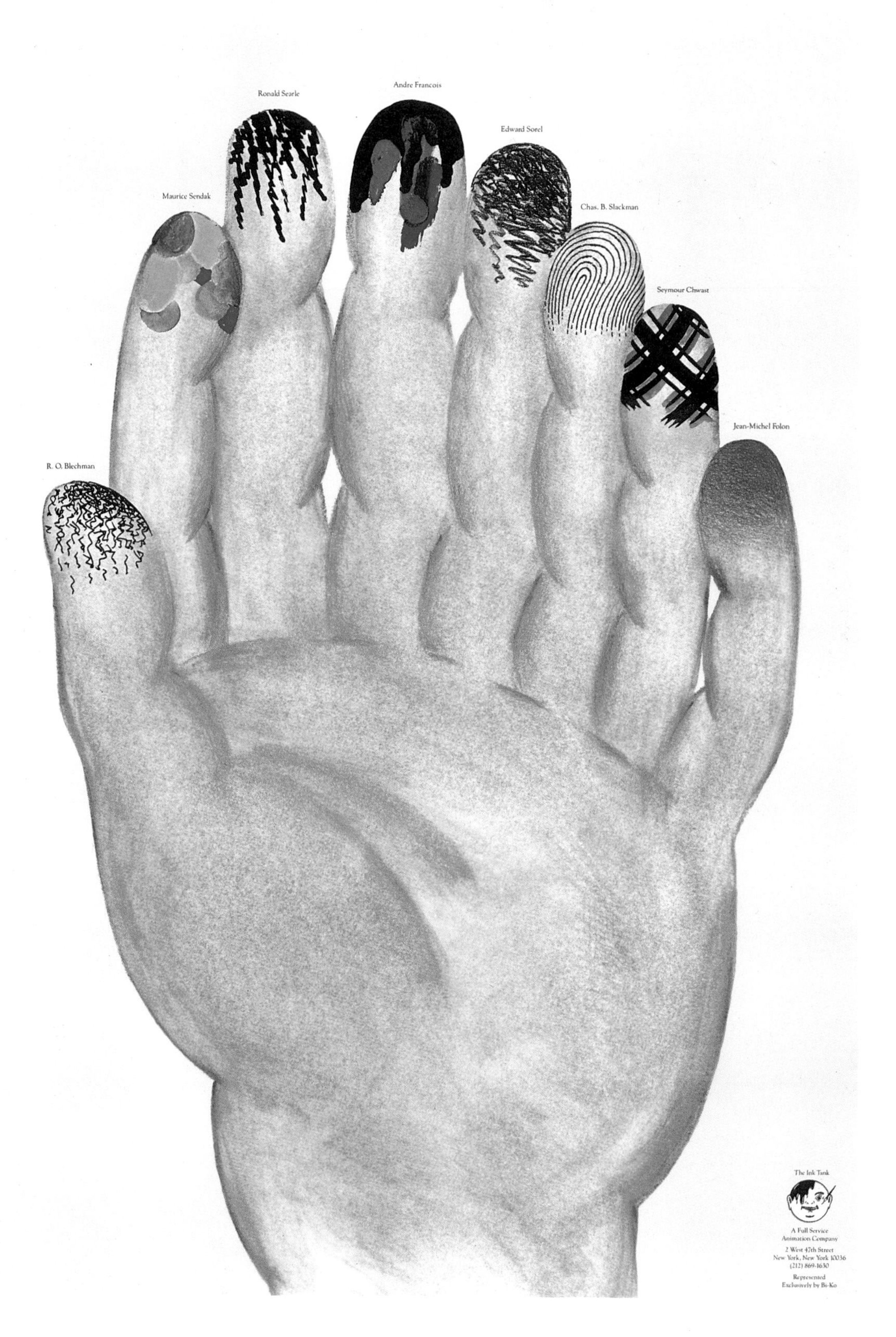

12

PERIDOT
Animation
Peridot Films, Inc. 222 E. 44 Street, New York 10017 212/867-8200 Jordan Caldwell Jack Dazzo

13

ELEKTRA
Elektra moves.
Elektra Film Productions moves to 501 Madison Avenue, New York 10022, PL 8-4830.

14

[15] For a cover of *New York* Magazine on European terrorism, I wanted to show the banality of terror: an embroidered ski mask, usually an accessory of innocent recreation, becomes the menacing silhouette of a terrorist.

The broadside and the poster are traditional media of protest. I am simply continuing the practice. [16] I designed *End Bad Breath* to protest the bombing of Hanoi during the Vietnam War. I took a mundane advertising slogan, married it to our most recognizable national symbol, and pushed the message home with an absurd but true idea. The blue plate is a woodcut; the flat colors were printed offset. [17] *War Is Good Business: Invest Your Son* was a common slogan printed on buttons during the Vietnam War. My version is a turn-of-the-century call to arms. [18] *March for Peace and Justice* was an assignment for the Peace March Committee—an announcement of the June 12, 1982 anti-nuke rally. The group asked me to do a positive image of peace, rather than a negative one of war, generally an easier approach. I rendered the dove, a timeworn but effective symbol, to suggest the notion that the marchers will come from different walks of life.

15

16

WAR
IS GOOD
BUSINESS
INVEST
YOUR
SON
Chwast

17

MARCH
JUNE 12
NEW YORK
FOR PEACE & JUSTICE
TO SUPPORT
THE UNITED NATIONS
SPECIAL SESSION ON
DISARMAMENT AND
TO CALL
FOR A FREEZE AND
REDUCTION OF ALL
NUCLEAR WEAPONS
AND A TRANSFER OF
MILITARY BUDGETS
TO HUMAN NEEDS.
JUNE 12
RALLY COMMITTEE
853 BROADWAY,
ROOM 2109
NEW YORK, N.Y. 10003
(212) 460-8980
LOCAL CONTACT:

18

[19] You don't have to be a cobbler to know that the perfect place in which to use a shoe is in a catalog advertising the Sony Walkman.

[20] In *Push Pin Moves*, the play is in the contrast of the large shape of the leg with the colorful shoe and shoelace.

[21] One image is as good as another for an exhibition poster. The rationale for the shoe in this case is that it vaguely symbolizes New York. The poster announced an exhibition of original illustrations in Munich.

19

20

Seymour Chwast
5.6.–28.7. 1984 Galerie Bartsch & Chariau Galeriestr. 2 8000 München 22
CHWAST

21

[22] This exhibition poster was inspired by a rendering of a fat butcher on a nineteenth-century poster. I have no idea what it was advertising, but the butcher's expanse of white apron suggested a vehicle for containing the lettering. I reasoned that I could use the same design for other exhibitions by just changing the blood-red text. To date, this was the only time it was used.

[23] The image of the friendly robot on the *Brooklyn Children's Museum* poster was originally designed as their trademark. I was smitten by the various mechanical devices made available for the kids to play with. I added the flowers in an effort to humanize the machine. A costume version has been used in parades.

[24] Olivetti asked Milton Glaser and me to design various printed materials for the 1968 Mexican Olympic Games, which they were sponsoring. I used a Mayan mask as my point of departure and made it round like the "O" in Olivetti. Shown here are the promotional mask and poster.

22

The Brooklyn Children's Museum
145 Brooklyn Avenue, Brooklyn, New York 11213 (212) 735-4400

23

OLIVETTI MEXICO 1968

24

[25] *Puccini* was designed to promote a New York festival of the composer's work. I was asked to portray the maestro as a dandy, as well as to illustrate the operas being performed. I took my stylistic signal from the period in which Puccini worked, and approximated the look of turn-of-the-century theatrical posters. Though posters and bus signs were printed, the festival failed to take place because the musicians went out on strike.

[26] The Art Institute of Fort Lauderdale is near the beach, and the environs are as much an attraction as the school's curriculum.

[27] This poster announced a motorcycling event near a canal in Central France. A European art director asked me to parody an old European poster, which seemed odd because there was no shortage of artists on the Continent familiar with the material. I thought it odd that he should choose an American until I realized that the entire history of visual sources is available to all of us through books and other media. I chose a Ludwig Hohlwein poster of a man on a bicycle as the model for this image, and I borrowed the surrealist concept from Magritte. I apologize for mixing Victorian lettering with the Deco logo.

25

26

LA VIREE SUPERBE
PEUGEOT
BALADE SAUVAGE ENTRE LES DEUX MERS
DU 24 AU 29 JUILLET
CHWAST

27

[28] The *Tyler Print Workshop* poster was done to show the quality of their printing. Since this was not intended as a billboard-type poster, but rather to be read close up, the small type was legible. I used Xerography to give the line an aquatint quality.

Someday someone may analyze why Freud is such a recurring theme in my work, or why art directors tend to give me such assignments. Here are a few examples: **[29]** Freud and dreams, promoting a printing paper; **[30]** Freud as the martyred spokesman for orthodox psychoanalysis for the *New York Times Magazine*; **[31]** Freud and cocaine, for the Op-Ed Page of the *New York Times*.

28

SIGMUND FREUD HAD IT.
Who could forget Freud (except maybe Jung)? If you want to be remembered try Union Camp's Williamsburg Offset.

29

30

31

PUSHPINOFF ULTIMATE
ALMOND ASSORTMENT
ALMOND PEARLS, MINT ALMONDS & BURNDT ALMONDS
NET WT 48 OZ
STRAWBERRY
Savories
GLORIOUS
GARDEN
DELUXE
FRUIT & NUT
ASSORTMENT
NITESPOTS
PUSHPINOFF
ALMOND
PEARLS
CANDY
LOVE DROPS
A PUSHPINOFF CANDY
RASPBERRY
SNOW
SWEETS
FROM FRANCE
AFTER COFFEE COFFEE
CHOCOLATE COATED
Espresso Beans
NET WEIGHT
9 oz
(255g)

32

[32] Here is a situation in which I was not only the art director and illustrator, but the client. Our candy business began when the studio packaged little black mints and rock candy together and sent it to clients as Christmas gifts. We called it "Caviar on Ice." The response was such that Phyllis Flood, who was our representative, suggested that there might be a real consumer market for a line of candy packaged in collectible tins. We decided to start the Pushpinoff Candy line and Phyllis took on the responsibility for marketing and promotion, finding sources for the candies and outlets for sales. Most of the tin or glass containers have printed labels. *Nitespots, Major Maize*, and *Glorious Garden* (an elephant who meets himself going around) are printed on the tin. I dealt with only the last two in the conventional way that packages should be designed—as three-dimensional objects. Packaging is challenging because it involves designing in three dimensions. When successful, a package has tangible charm, in addition to its function.

[33] Illustrated riddles gave kids something to do while eating the Big Macs that came in this carton.

[34] Department stores often stack boxes of glassware on the selling floor to display them. The rounded ends of these cartons add a deco sculptural quality. The more expensive line, *Charmont*, has a silver background. While most packages of this kind carry photographs of glasses, this illustrative and typographic approach distinguishes itself from the competition.

[35] Only after I designed the "a" did someone say it looked like a drop of ink. It's funny how fresh eyes perceive unconscious meanings. The box design was applied to the bottle label and carton.

[36] This art deco monogram was designed for an elegant boutique in Paris, where the art of shopping bags is at a high level of sophistication.

33

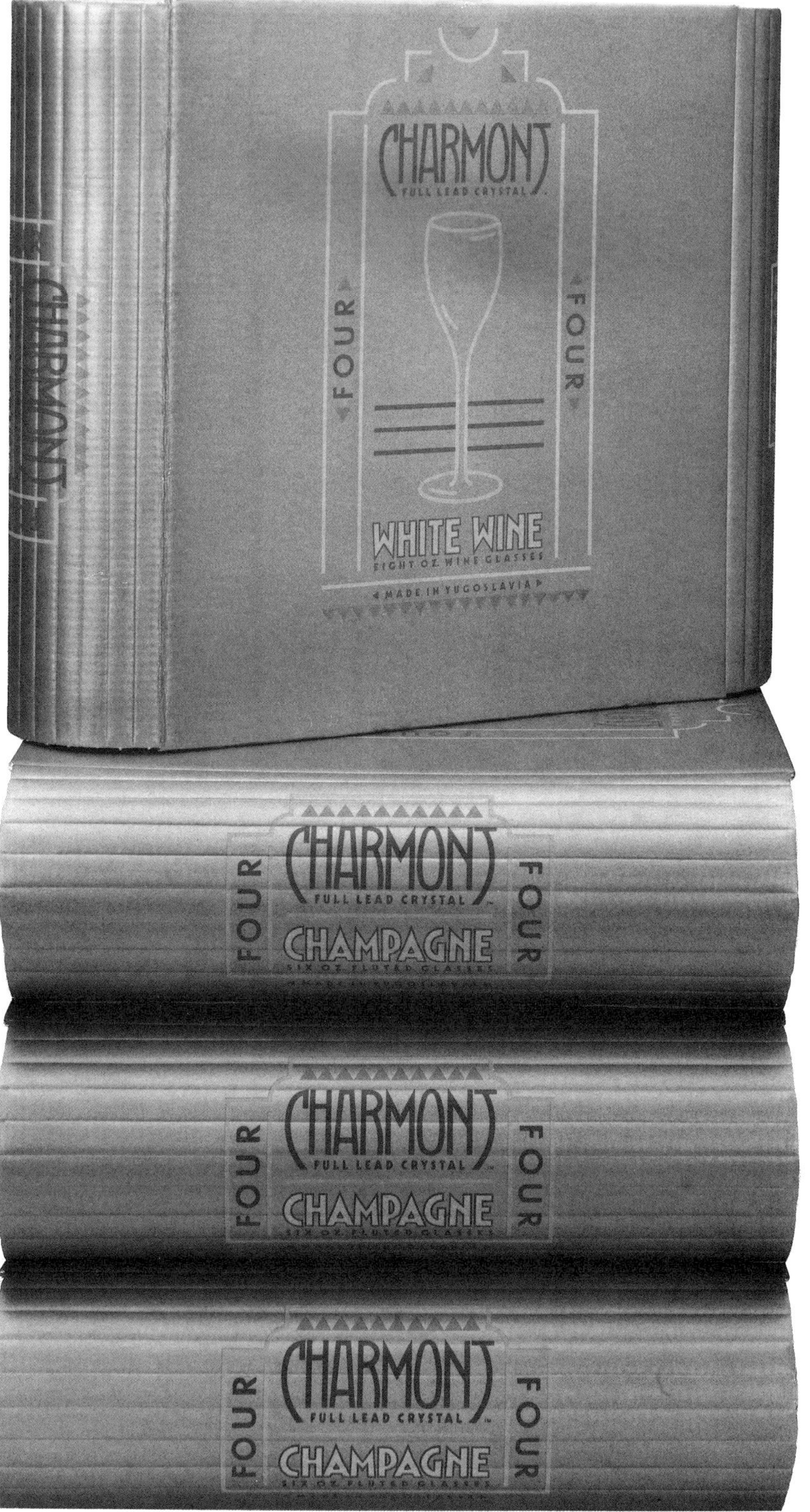

34

AVALLON
FOUR
FOUR
WHITE WINE
EIGHT OZ. WINE GLASSES
FINE STEMWARE
AVALLON
FOUR
CHAMPAGNE
AVALLON
FOUR
CHAMPAGNE

Artone
Studio India
Ink

35

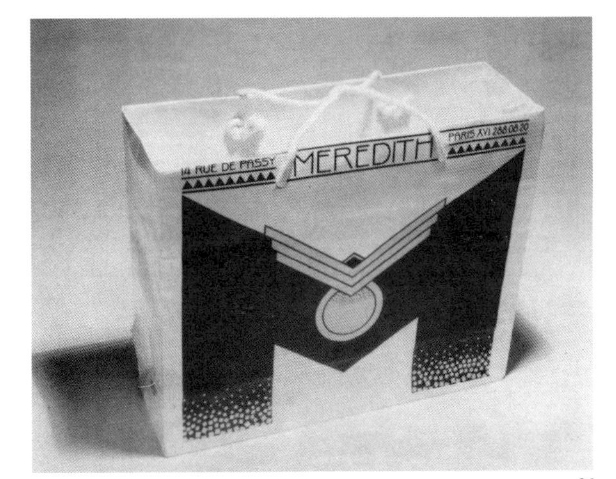
14 RUE DE PASSY
MEREDITH
PARIS XVI 288.08.20

36

[37] I was asked to design the box for a new "family-style" cereal, showing the family as well as a large illustration of the product. The bowl of cereal is pictured as a hooked rug on top of which the "folk art" family is having its breakfast. My cleverness could not overcome a market test that failed; the package was not produced.

[38] The concept for Erlanger Beer came from Norman Black, the art director of the company's ad agency. Since the brewing method was 400 years old, a traditional but elaborate label and carton were employed to convey Old World quality. Several artists supplied the engraving-style illustrations.

[39] This assignment involved developing the names of a group of houseware products as well as a format for their packages. Two color schemes were devised to differentiate between the copperware and the wood products. The cigar band device changed its shape to accommodate renderings of the products.

37

38

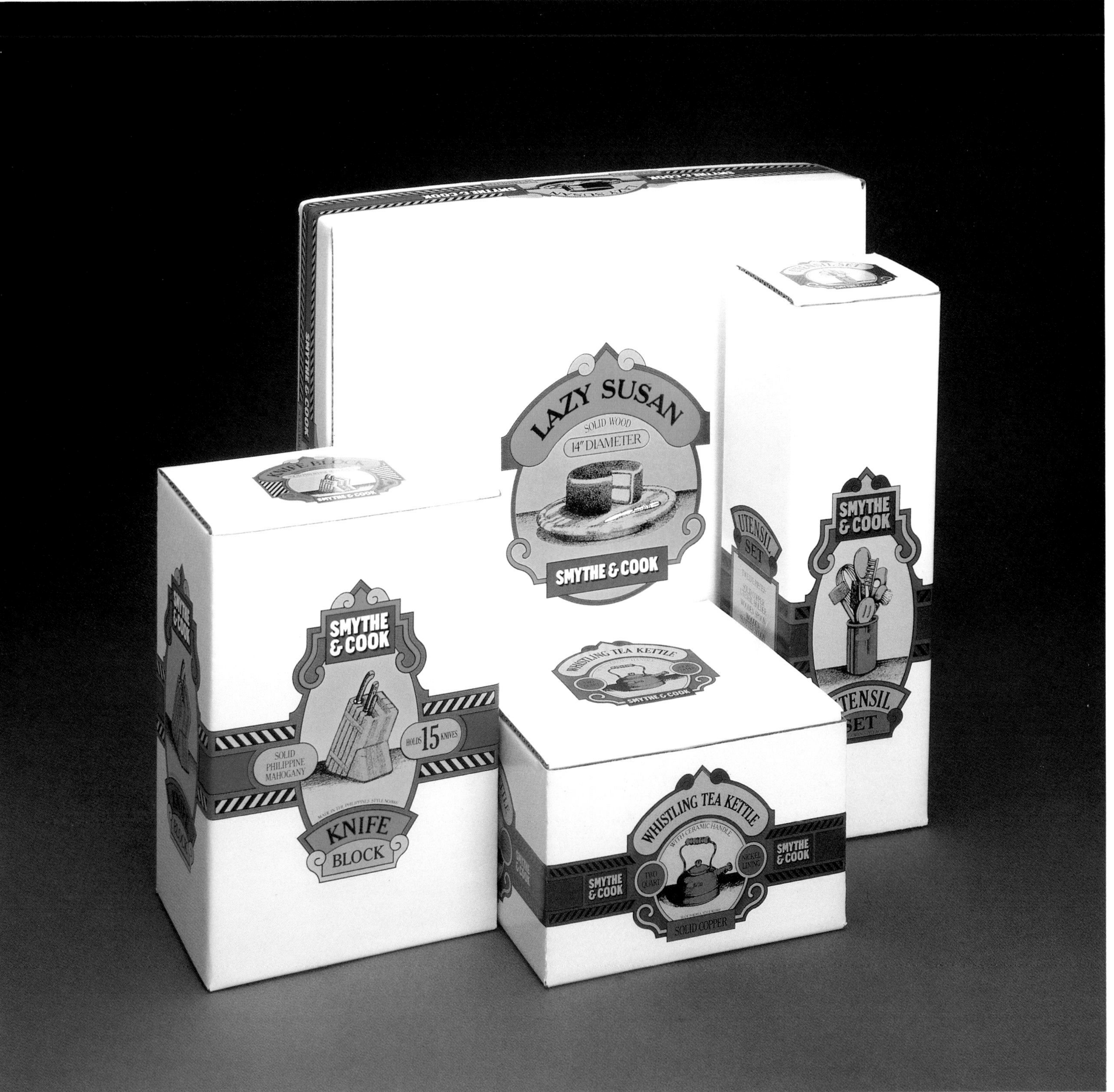
LAZY SUSAN
SOLID WOOD
14" DIAMETER
SMYTHE & COOK
UTENSIL
SET
SMYTHE
& COOK
UTENSIL
SET
SMYTHE
& COOK
SOLID
PHILIPPINE
MAHOGANY
HOLDS 15 KNIVES
KNIFE
BLOCK
WHISTLING TEA KETTLE
SMYTHE & COOK
WHISTLING TEA KETTLE
WITH CERAMIC HANDLE
SMYTHE
& COOK
TWO
QUART
NICKEL
LINING
SMYTHE
& COOK
SOLID COPPER

The function of a trademark is to be memorable. **[40]** The comic moon face used for the *Ink Tank* was curiously self-effacing, but not without charm. **[41]** *Lörke* is a German men's and women's fashion chain. I designed the logo to reflect the look of their Art Nouveau building, and the smart-aleckey cat was meant to suggest sophistication. I liked the cat; the client didn't. Instead, they are using a fleur-de-lys with my logotype. **[42]** The Push Pin Chicken was originally designed as a symbol for the "Chicken!" issue of the *Push Pin Graphic*. We kept it as our mascot.

[43] *Nickelodeon* was a company that produced music for film and television. The mark on this letterhead speaks for itself.

[44] From the original Push Pin logos, designed with Reynold Ruffins and Milton Glaser, it was a long leap to the contemporary monogram. The geometric look represented the increasingly corporate nature of the studio.

40

41

42

Nickelodeon
INC.
MUSIC
430 Park AVE.
New York
10022
(212) 753-9883

43

44

[45] The idea for this cover of a brochure for a health club came from its title, *Biofitness Inside and Out*. When the translucent cover is opened, it reveals the man and the woman in their skivvies. Each spread introduces a different service offered by the club. I designed the brochure and art-directed the work of several illustrators for the interior. Shown here is my contribution.

The Exercise Addict

Case Study

Chief Complaint:

- ☐ "Exercise is my passion, but I've done it all. I'm looking for a fresh, new approach to fitness."
- ☐ "I love pushing myself to the limit, but maybe I can go further with a professional."
- ☐ "When it comes to fitness, I want the ultimate— I'm tired of *shopping*. Where do I find all the best under one roof?"
- ☐ "I exercise as much as my friend but she's the one who looks great with toned muscles and energy that won't quit!…What's *she* doing right?"
- ☐ "Fitness is a science. I want to know exactly how fit I am, but where do I find the latest technology and the experts who know how to use it?"
- ☐ "I never miss a workout, but it's tough to let go and relax…I wish I could get both at once."
- ☐ "I'm a serious athlete. Off-season training is the key to in-season performance. I need a program geared for me."

Objective:

New Dimensions: Experience exciting, new ways to exercise as your personal trainer guides you through a unique system of equipment and programs specially designed to achieve your specific fitness goals.
Expert Consultation: Push yourself to ever expanding limits as our professional staff keeps you working at optimal levels of performance and safety.
Complete Facility: Find the newest equipment, innovative programs, and expert staff to meet all your fitness needs.
Individualized Attention: Work with your personal trainer to establish a fitness program that gets the results you want.
Technologically Advanced: Find out how fit you are and what your next best step should be as our highly trained staff employs a sophisticated, scientifically conceived system for conditioning.
Total Approach: When you've finished working out you're not finished yet. Complete your conditioning program; relax and re-energize in a *forgotten dimension of fitness.*
Serious Program: Improve high level performance with a certified athletic trainer who creates a program to meet your specialized training objectives.

Prescription:

Biofitness Individualized Conditioning Program

■ **Fitness Evaluation**
In your case, a complete *Fitness Evaluation* keys especially on these areas:
Personal Health Behavior Profile—because how you live outside Biofitness determines your program inside.
Cardiorespiratory Evaluation—because performance in your conditioning program depends on the capacity to maintain high levels of cardiorespiratory function, our exercise physiologist measures oxygen uptake, calories burned, and target heart rate, on the computer assisted *Dynavit* Ergometer to determine your most effective, safest aerobic training program.
Structural Analysis—because highly trained individuals need a clear understanding of posture, gait, range of motion, and muscle strength, for greater efficiency in strenuous exercise and everyday living, our physical therapist performs a comprehensive musculoskeletal evaluation.
Hydrostatic Weighing—because you want to know your exact body fat, our exercise physiologist accurately determines your body composition by comparing your weight in water to your weight on land.
Periodic Retesting—because you deserve to know how you're doing and because we need accurate information about your progress to keep your conditioning program precisely focused on your goals.

■ **Flexibility Training**
Harmony between strength and flexibility is essential for high level performance. Flexibility Instructors work closely with you to maximize flexibility and minimize risk of injury as you push yourself to safe limits.

■ **Aerobic Training**
The combined function of your heart, lungs and circulatory system are your foundation for high level performance. Our exercise physiologist helps create challenging individualized programs that provide incentives for reaching new goals. Enjoy the new Biobike and Versa-Climber in addition to Fitron Ergometers, computerized Marquette Treadmills and a range of other aerobic apparatus.

■ **Strength Training**
The *Fitness Evaluation* and your personal strength building objectives help your trainer create a progressive resistance training program designed for optimal results. Strengthen and tone in a sophisticated system including Nautilus, Universal, Cam-II pneumatics, York Olympic Free Weights, Total Gym, Hydragym, and the Cybex Orthotron.

■ **Relaxation Training**
Experience the total fitness spectrum. Relaxation, *a forgotten dimension of fitness*, completes the Biofitness conditioning continuum. Relax and re-energize in *steam showers* and special *therapeutic whirlpools*, float in *Samadhi Tanks*, or choose from a variety of massage techniques offered by *licensed Massage Therapists.*

■ **Special Services**
An unusual selection of fitness alternatives complement your case study. Our *licensed Nutritionist* offers a course in "Eating For Athletes," as well as individualized programs for weight loss or weight gain that *define what works for you and what you can live with.* Extend your conditioning program to include a combination dance/calisthenics or aerobic martial arts *Movement Class.*

SEYMOUR CHWAST

15

[46] What intrigued me in making this drawing for an article on health clubs for the *Frankfurter Allgemeine Magazin* was the contrast of the large and small shapes of the machine and their relationship to the body's muscles. I drew this with colored pencil and acrylic on heavy, textured, dark brown paper, which I then cut out and pasted on a pale background.

Männer mit Muskeln: Der Health Club verspricht Gesundheit für Sieger, den Körper als Kunstwerk bis hinein ins hohe Alter

Schweiß muß fließen. In Downtown Manhattan treten Wallstreet-Banker keuchend in computergesteuerte Standradpedale, vor sich auf dem Lenkrad die „Business Week" und über sich Monitore mit Börsennachrichten. Midtown, im Ambiente spiegelglitzernder Diskotheken, disziplinieren sich junge Aufsteiger festgeschnallt auf weißgepolsterten Foltermaschinen. Der Restaurantkritiker der „Washington Post" berichtet längst über Fitness-Center und Diät-Hotels, in denen die Opfer des städtischen Luxus freudig ihren öl- und salzfreien Salat mit nichts als einer eisgekühlten Gabel genießen. Selbst die Intellektuellen von Greenwich Village haben die Lust am Bewegen der Massen verloren und kümmern sich beim workout um ihre eigene Physis. Vorbei die Zeiten von Protestliedern und Protestmärschen. Drogen und Hippies sind Legenden aus der Vergangenheit wie Woodstock oder nächtelange Diskussionen in verräucherten Kneipen. Jetzt sprechen die Körper.

SCHWITZE NARZISS!

Von Brigitte Scherer
Illustrationen Seymour Chwast

26

48

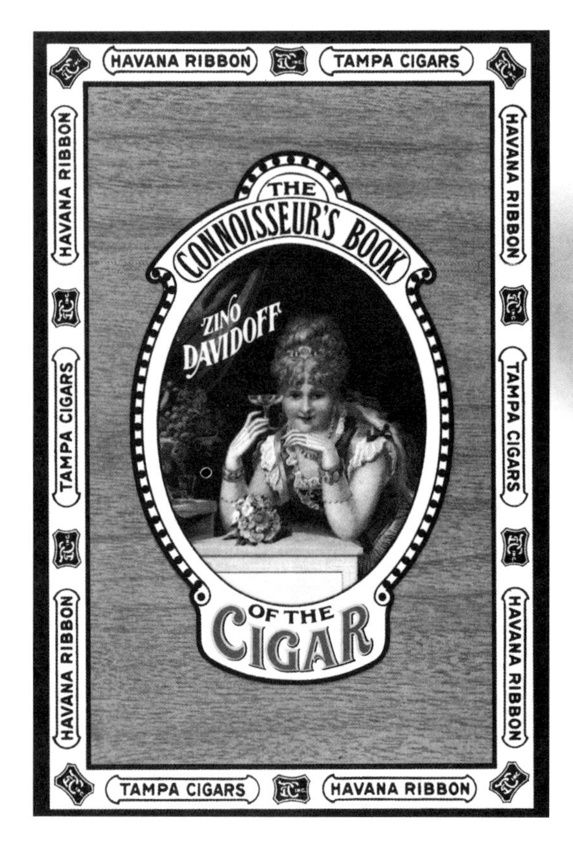

THE CONNOISSEUR'S BOOK OF

THE

Cigar.

BY

Z. Davidoff

WITH THE
COLLABORATION OF
GILLES LAMBERT

TRANSLATED
FROM THE FRENCH BY
LAWRENCE GROW

McGraw-Hill

BOOK COMPANY
NEW YORK
ST. LOUIS
SAN FRANCISCO
TORONTO
MEXICO CITY
PANAMA

47

[47] In an effort to make *The Connoisseur's Book of the Cigar* as much like a cigar box as possible, I used a border from an actual cigar box, some wood grain printed paper, an old Victorian chromolith as a centerpiece, and hand lettering. The inside cover was made to look like the real thing, and the first page was a drawing of cigars lying in the box. I used the "Lady Mary's" cigar band as a design accent on the title page.

[48] The editorial material dictated the design of *The Sweet Heart & Others.* A pocket-sized book, it showed the heart in every possible form: as playing cards, typographic devices, a bathtub for a Pocono resort, ice cream pop, men's underwear, and last but not least, the human organ.

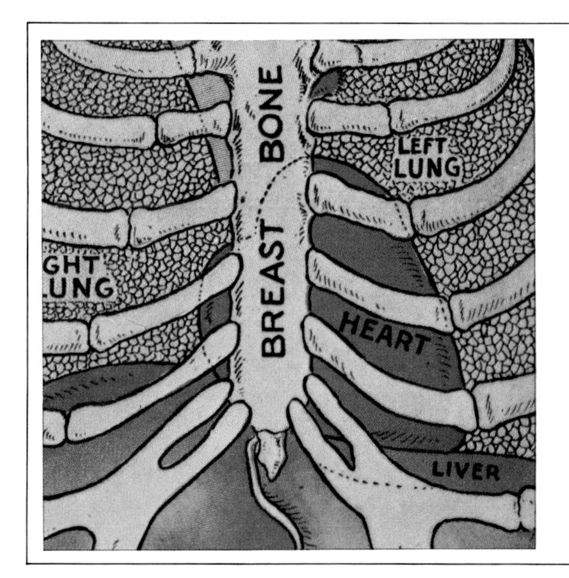

FLARE BOOKS
PUBLISHED BY
AVON

8

16

19

49

[49] When I was asked to design *The One Show Annual*, it was a paperback—a poor cousin to the *Art Directors Annual*. The only constraint was that I had to use their symbol, the double-ended pencil—one point representing copy and the other art. Not a bad image, and a good point of departure. Each year the problem was to render it differently, in style and form. I've done five, in collaboration with Richard Mantel and Michael Aron. Also shown here are divider pages that continue the cover motif.

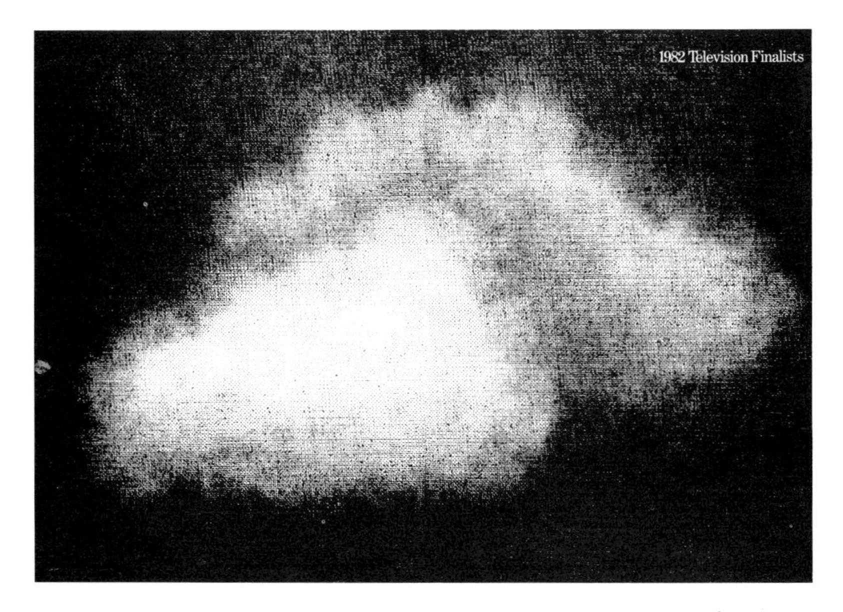

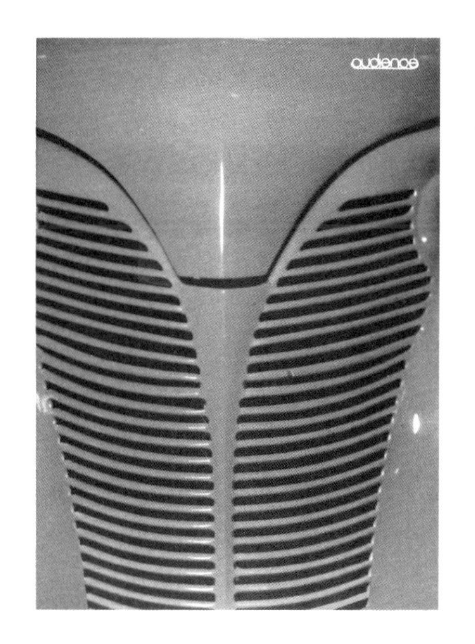

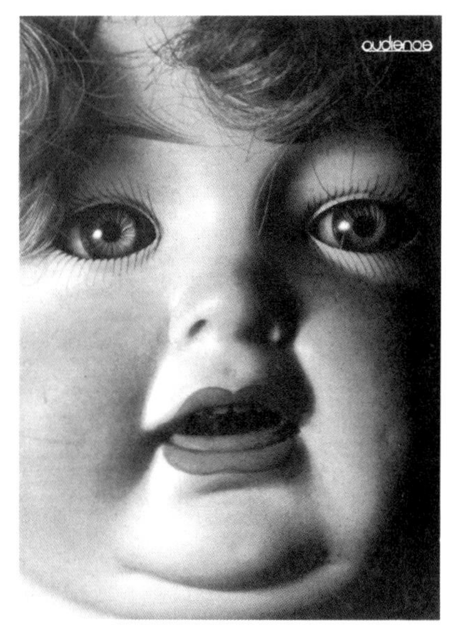

[50] There was no advertising in *Audience* magazine, a hardcover periodical devoted to art and culture. Milton Glaser and I were the art directors, with more than the usual freedom. The binding style made *Audience* something between a book and a magazine, and we designed accordingly. Not having ads to interfere with editorial matter is unique in magazines. Because *Audience* wasn't sold on newsstands, we were able to use a smaller logo without any cover-lines. It was hoped that a high cover price would eliminate the need for advertising to make the magazine a success; regrettably, the experiment failed.

[51] I did these wrappers for a story in *Audience* magazine on the Hershey's candy company. While the brand names were real, my designs were imaginary, based on whim and American pop package design.

[52] For *Rolling Stone*, I was asked to invent names and create packages for legalized marijuana cigarettes. Using a combination of collage and illustration, my overall design was based on those wonderful tobacco shop advertising placards, on which real packages are glued.

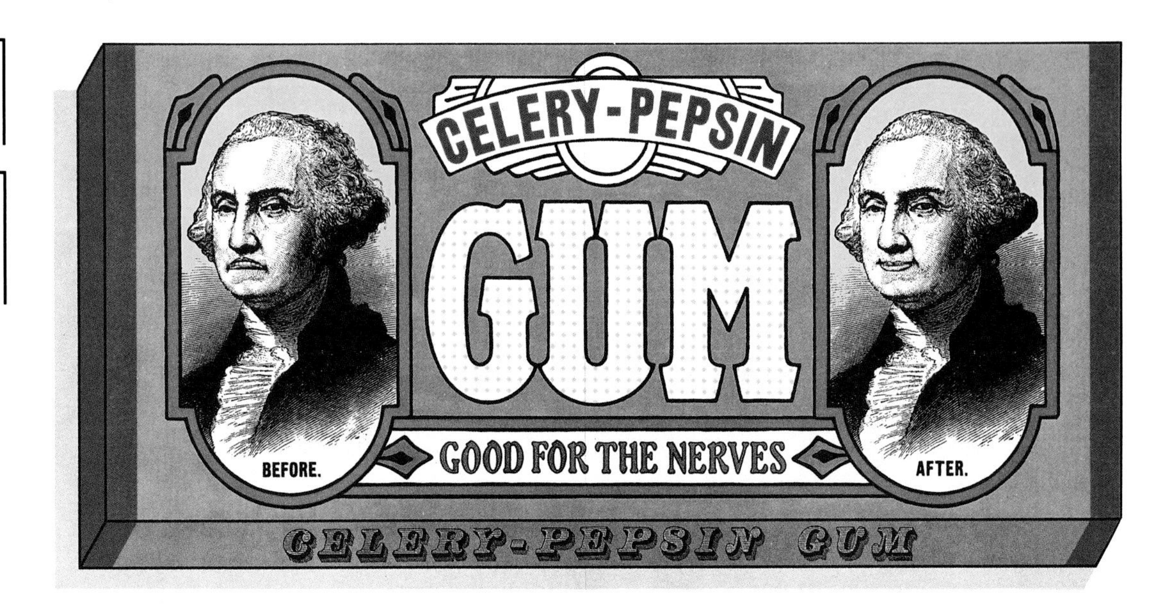

51

The World's Finest
HIGH SIERRA
KANSAS CITY
KINGS
ACAPULCO
GOLD
A PROMISE IN EVERY PUFF
MORE PLEASURE PER TOKE
MONTEGO BAY
IN GOD WE TRUST
OLD Saigon
Smooth Sailing
CHWAST
52

I enjoy designing books, particularly those that I have contributed to as an editor. **[53]** *The Art of New York* is a tribute to the city through its art. Designed with an overall deco sensibility, it uses Cheltenham, a vigorous non-deco typeface that seems to work with everything I do. The type style also kept the book from becoming too elegant. **[54]** *Art Against War* is a survey of 400 years of protest in art. The type is set in Bodoni Book for text, with Kabel Bold headlines. **[55]** *The Illustrated Flower* reflects my love of catalogues, for this was a lavish, annotated compendium of the world's flora. I used Goudy Old Style for the text and Goudy Handtooled for the heads.

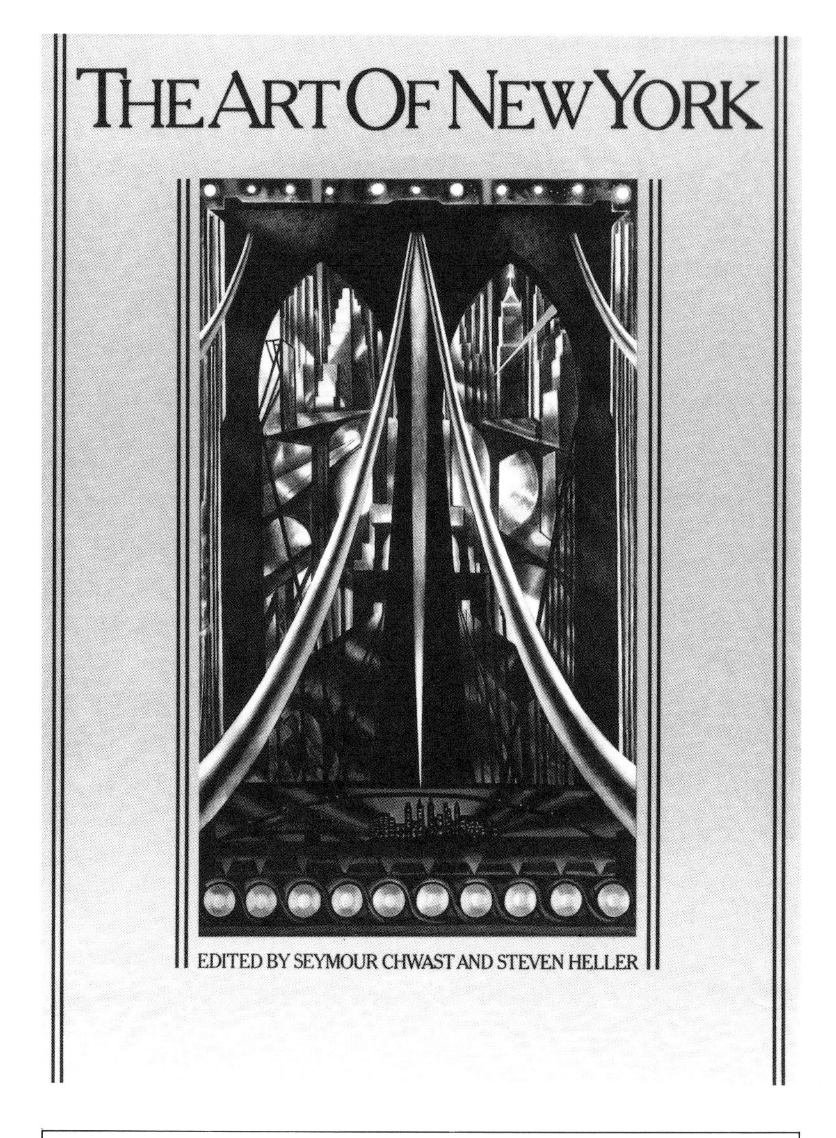

Robert Cottingham. *Rat*. 1978. Oil on canvas, 78" x 78". Private collection
Courtesy Coe Kerr Gallery, New York City

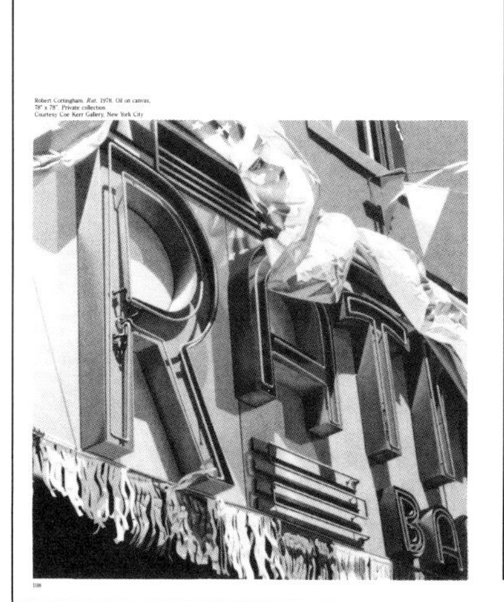

On any person who desires such queer prizes, New York will bestow the gift of loneliness and the gift of privacy.
E. B. White
Here Is New York

53

ART AGAINST WAR
D.J.R. BRUCKNER SEYMOUR CHWAST STEVEN HELLER

THE ILLUSTRATED
Flower
BY SEYMOUR CHWAST
& EMILY BLAIR CHEWNING

SOCIALIST ATOMIC REALISM
РАЗОРЪЖЕТЕ СЕ !

NIE!

Dahlia
TRAVAXA
HAILLICHACRAIAPUIE
TRAVAXO
ZARATARPVMITAI
TRAVAXA
CHACRAMATAPISCO
August
September
October

1726-1733 Bach fructified.

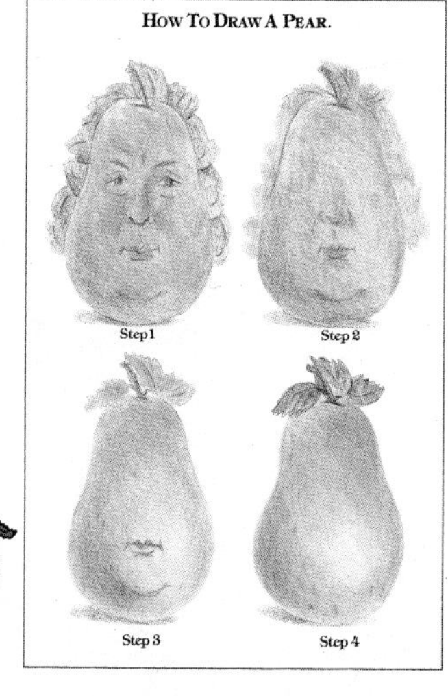

1734 Commedia del Bach.

1750 The death of Bach.

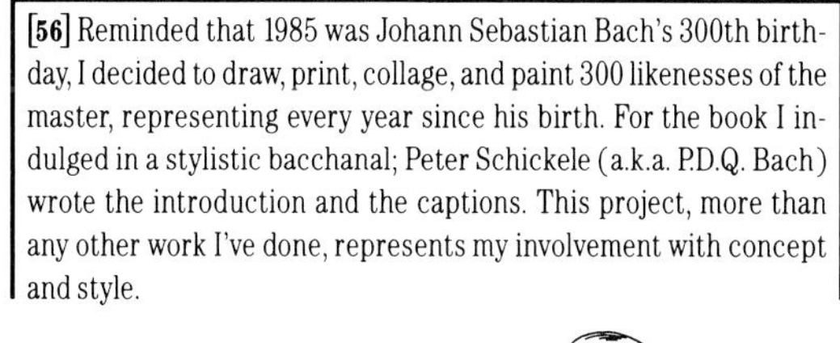

[56] Reminded that 1985 was Johann Sebastian Bach's 300th birthday, I decided to draw, print, collage, and paint 300 likenesses of the master, representing every year since his birth. For the book I indulged in a stylistic bacchanal; Peter Schickele (a.k.a. P.D.Q. Bach) wrote the introduction and the captions. This project, more than any other work I've done, represents my involvement with concept and style.

1913, 1914 Bach with wheels.

1962 D. D. D. Bach.

1963 Bach is beautiful.

[57] *The Sophisticated Traveler* cover was inspired by the 1930s poster artist A.M. Cassandre, who created the Dubonnet man. The cover went through a number of incarnations: first it was only a man, then the editors insisted on including a woman. Next, they "encouraged" me to make the labels larger. I'm afraid that the oversized labels diminished the idea of the man's body as a suitcase.

[58] My appreciation of the past helped me do the illustration for "Whatever Happened to Father?," a cover for the *New York Times Magazine*. Here my inspiration was the graphic genius Ludwig Hohlwein, the leading German poster artist of the 1930s, who was known for reducing an image to its essential elements. In this case, the flat pattern defines the chair, not the outline. The chair is the dominant image, framing an invisible father. I subsequently produced the design in a silkscreen print, as shown here.

57

58

59

[59] Usually there is little time for tinkering with a *Time* cover because the deadlines are so short. In fact, *Time* commissions several artists for different covers each week, so I'm not only competing with other designs or with photographs, but also with world events. In this case, the news peg was the fall of the Shah of Iran. It was imminent, and the idea to do him as a Persian carpet came quickly. However, because his collapse took longer than expected, the cover was repeatedly postponed. During that time, the editors played with a number of variations on my idea, for example, burning the corners of the carpet. The moment finally came, however, and the cover ran as originally planned, but only on the International Edition. For the national *Time*, they used something else.

[60] This cover for the *Atlantic* illustrates the notion that the presence of police stabilizes inner-city neighborhoods. [61] For an *Atlantic* cover story called "Living with the Bomb," I did a dead-pan farce. The art director suggested that I literally show an American family at home with a bomb. By emphasizing the realistic, nonsymbolic details of the room, the matter-of-factness of the bomb itself was heightened.

[62] The covers for *New York* Magazine's "Fall Previews" shown here are two of the five that I've done. In addition to being a roundup of the season's events, each issue had a different theme, such as "Rites of Spring" and "Gossip," shown here.

60

CHWAST

61

New York
50 CENTS
SEPTEMBER 11, 1972
FALL CATALOGUE
SECRETS OF THE FALL REVEALED
Sports
Music
Books
Plays
Gossip!
AVOID BOREDOM
INCREASE JOY
Fashion
Art & Dance
Movies
Television
Predictions! The Low-Down! Insider Reports!

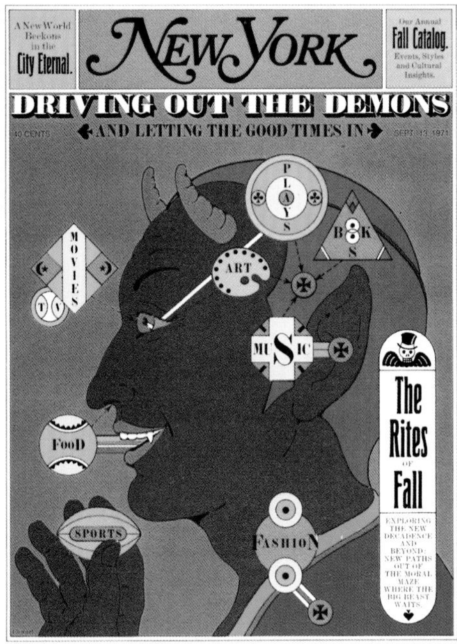
A New World Beckons in the City Eternal.
New York
Our Annual Fall Catalog. Events, Styles and Cultural Insights.
DRIVING OUT THE DEMONS
AND LETTING THE GOOD TIMES IN
PLAYS
BOOKS
MOVIES
TV
ART
MUSIC
FOOD
SPORTS
FASHION
The Rites of Fall
EXPLORING THE NEW DECADENCE AND BEYOND: NEW PATHS OUT OF THE MORAL MAZE WHERE THE BIG BEAST WAITS.

62

[63] My interest in mail order catalogues prompted this cover for an *Idea* magazine issue devoted to my work. The pen points came from a page in a catalogue, and I collaged some of the shafts. I'm amused by the often arbitrary and romantic names that car manufacturers and real estate developers give their products to give them allure. I did it here, too.

[64] "The Marriage of Art and Literature on Their Wedding Night" was a *Graphis* cover. It was done in colored pencil and acrylic on chipboard.

[65] This poster promoting *The Writer's New York City Source Book* is an ideal solution because the pen and skyscraper—stereotypes for both writers and New York—can be expressed in the same image. (See also *The Death Ship*, page 65.)

63

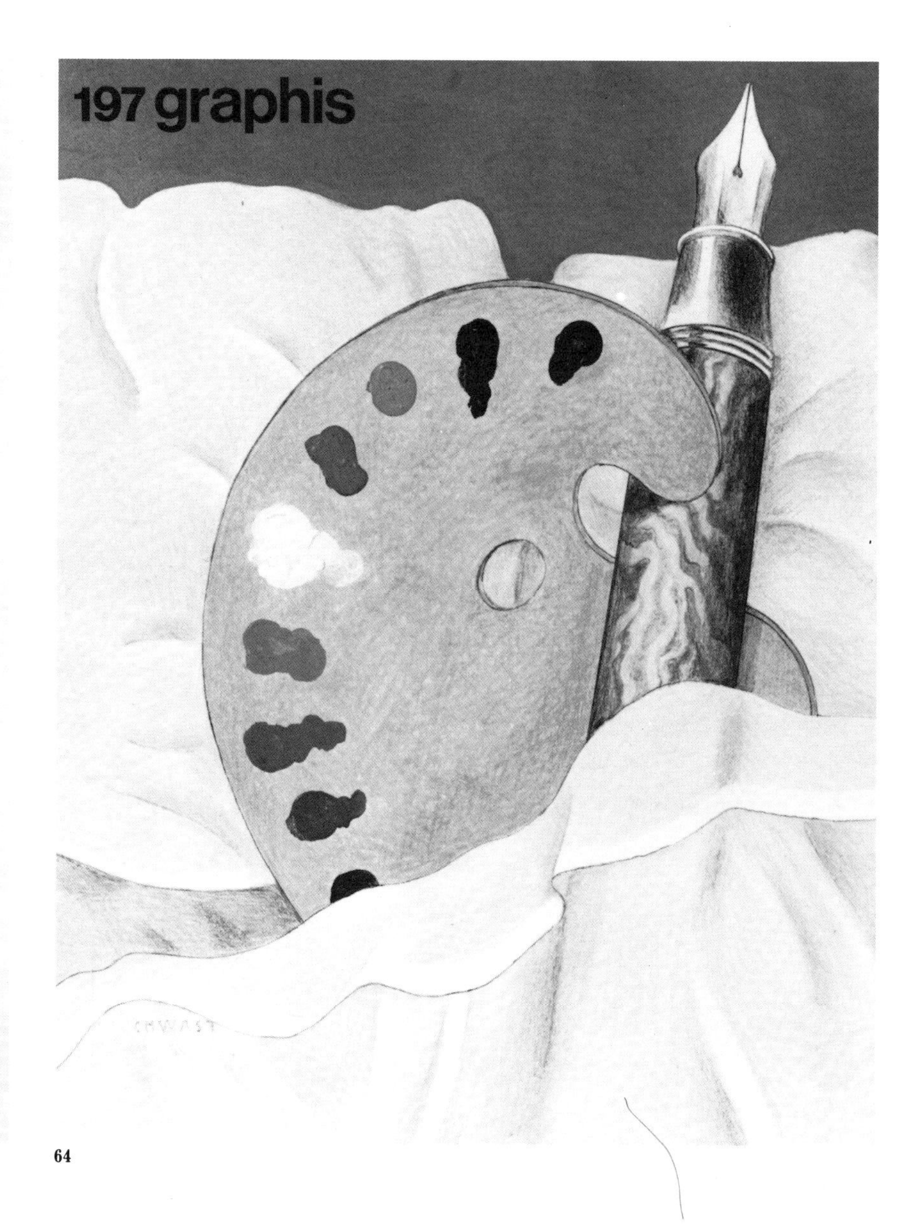

64

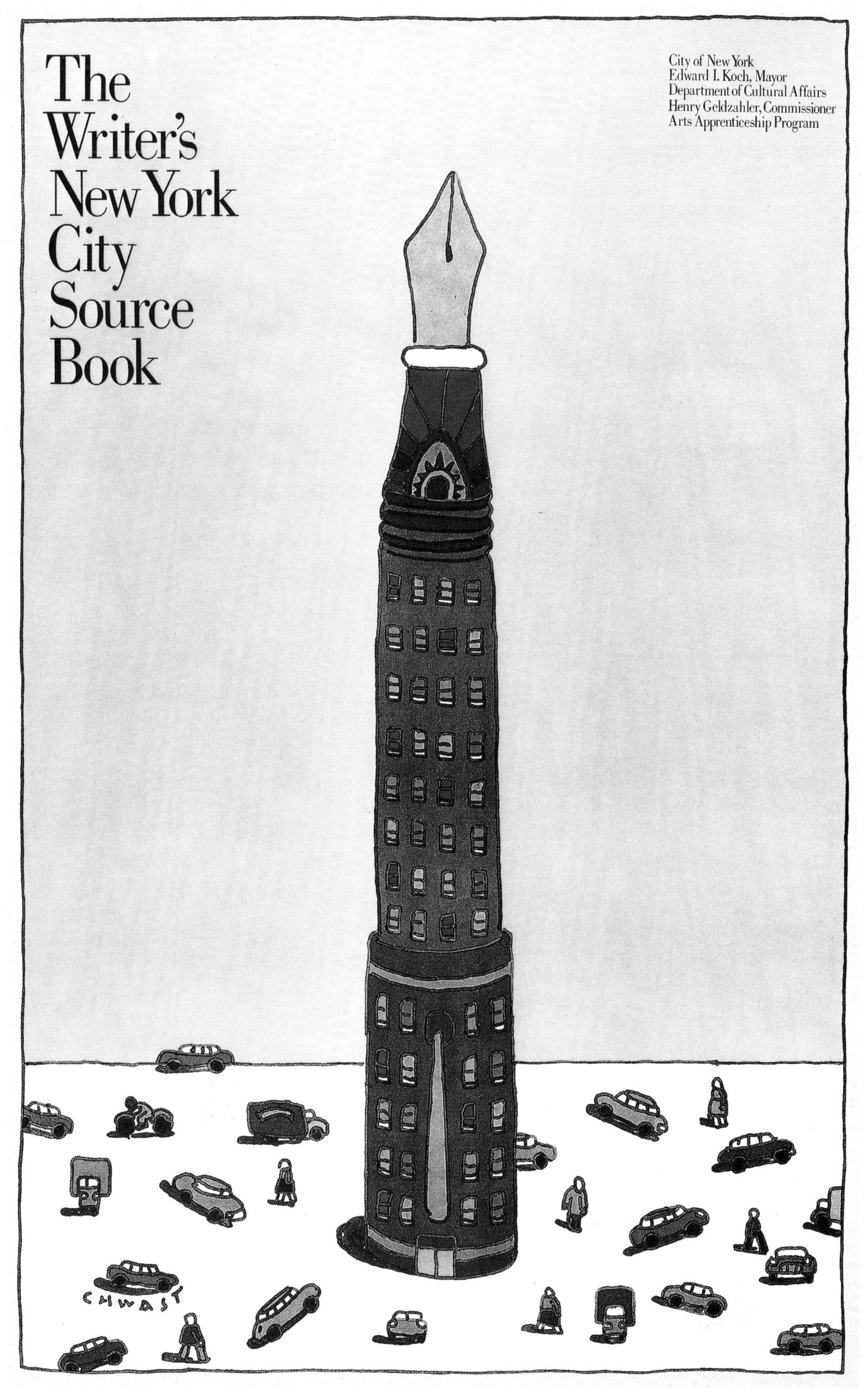
The
Writer's
New York
City
Source
Book
City of New York
Edward I. Koch, Mayor
Department of Cultural Affairs
Henry Geldzahler, Commissioner
Arts Apprenticeship Program
CHWAST

The book jacket is an excellent arena for the designer who likes to draw. **[66]** *The Grand Tour* is a book about the lively travel exploits of European aristocrats during the eighteenth century. I thought it appropriate to do a robust drawing in the style of Rowlandson and Gillray, two of England's leading satirists of the period. **[67]** *The Death Ship* was one of my earliest paperback covers. Done in pen-and-ink, it is a successful solution to the common problem of having to convey two ideas in one image. **[68]** *Zorba the Greek* was done as a monoprint because the style reflected the vigor of the hero. **[69]** The illustration for *Nocturnal Vaudeville* was one of the few jobs I've done in ballpoint pen. I enjoyed the looseness of the medium, which allowed for more modelling than I usually do.

66

The Death Ship
$.95
B.TRAVEN
"An unforgettable novel, a devastating attack
on bureaucracy and the state; an ironic, compassionate
unrivaled picture of homeless seamen"—RAMPARTS MAGAZINE

67

Nikos Kazantzakis
AN ESSANDESS PAPERBACK $1.95
ZorbA
The Greek

68

69

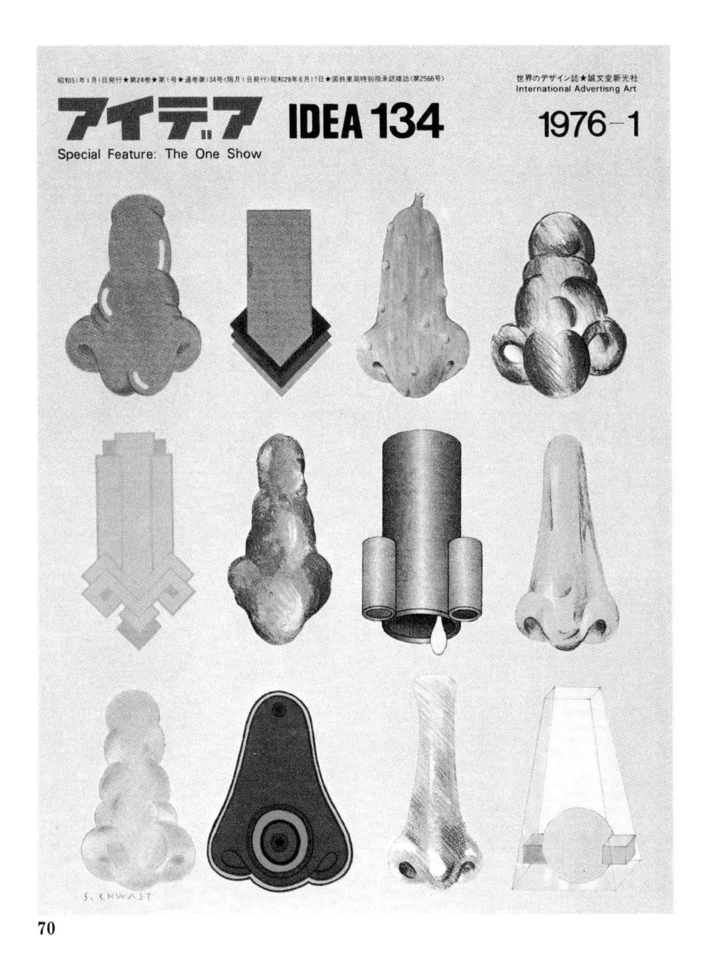
世界のデザイン誌★誠文堂新光社
International Advertisng Art
アイデア IDEA 134
1976-1
Special Feature: The One Show
S. CHWAST

70

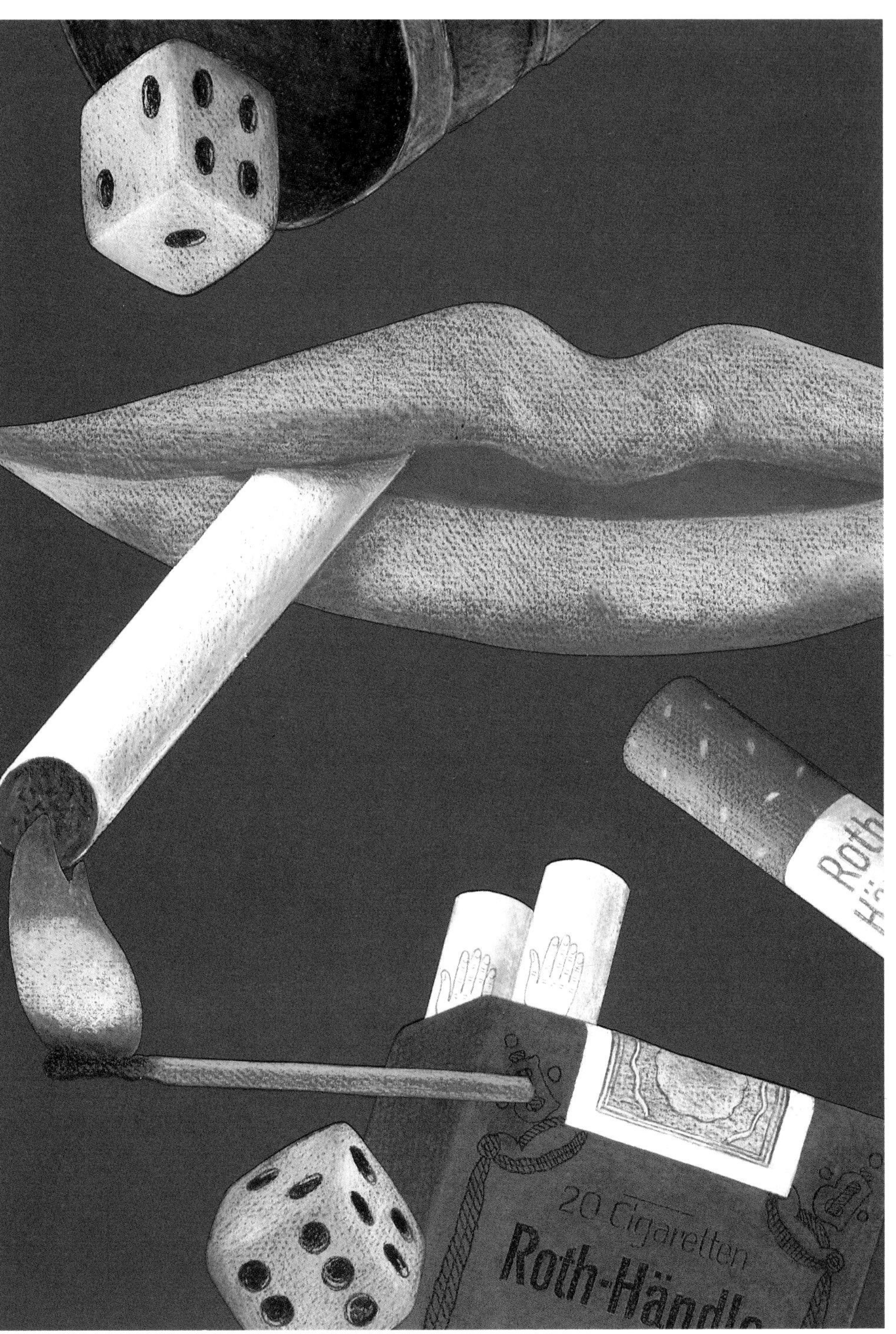
Roth
20 Cigaretten
Roth-Händl

71

73

72

[70] Since I enjoy serial images (what I sometimes call catalogues) and working in different styles, this cover of *Idea* magazine was a perfect opportunity to do both. Choosing noses was part satire and part idolatry.

[71] This is my unsound (and unpublished) ad for a German cigarette—one they called the workingman's cigarette. I rendered it in colored pencil on textured paper, making the lips very posterlike. The curious part of this job was that the client asked me to use the dice. While the Germans equate the image only with recreation, the dice remind an American that smoking is gambling with your health.

[72] The cover for *Graphis 175* was pegged to an article on my exhibition "100 Heads of Seymour Chwast." I executed it with cut construction paper; the only drawing is in the smoke and some shading between the teeth.

[73] For the *Graphis Poster Annual* I looked at previous covers, all of them using a stark single poster. To be unexpected, I chose to tell a story, and made an unposterlike illustration of a burglar who breaks into a room and steals the poster hanging on the wall, ignoring a woman sleeping in bed. As source material I borrowed the furniture and acid colors in a room from a postcard advertising a motel—Cozy Cabin Camp—in Georgia.

[74] *Passenger* is a novel narrated by an extroverted, English-speaking fetus. The idea for the jacket was full born in my head.

The two versions of *How To Do Things Right* exemplify how different are hardcover and paperback marketing strategies. [75] is a more complicated composition with a subtle idea, while [76] has a more immediate impact for the paperback rack.

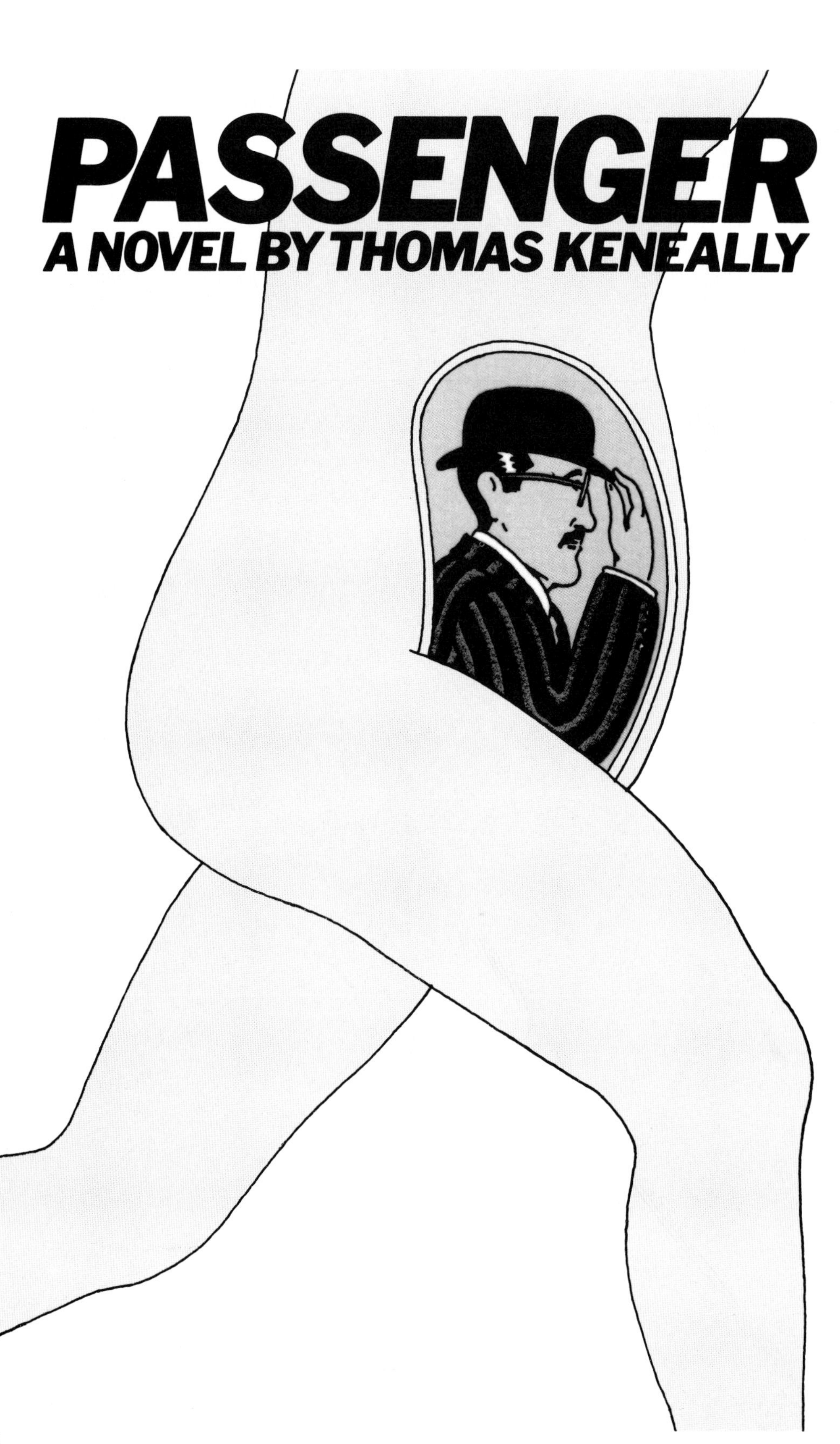

74

HOW TO DO THINGS RIGHT

The Revelations of a Fussy Man by L. Rust Hills

Chwast

75

76

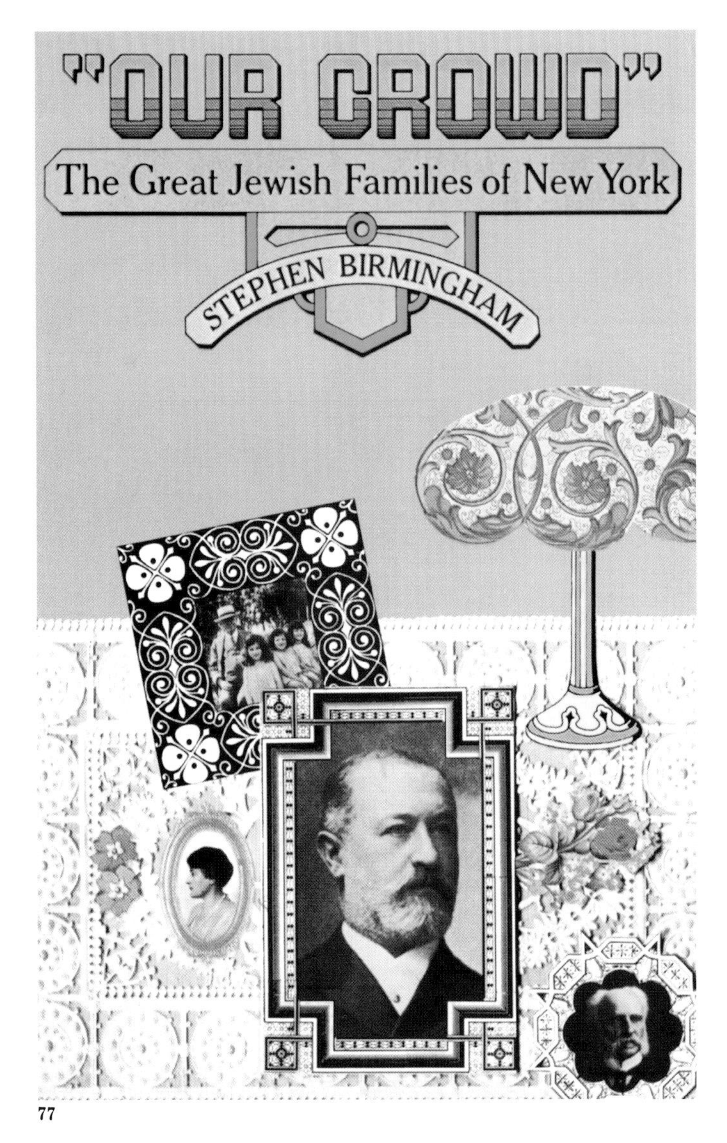
"OUR CROWD"
The Great Jewish Families of New York
STEPHEN BIRMINGHAM

77

CORVO
SAINT OR MADMAN?
A New Biography of Frederick William Rolfe
By Donald Weeks
CHWAST

78

The Yellow Book
An Illustrated Quarterly
Volume II July 1894
London: Elkin Mathews & John Lane
Boston: Copeland & Day
Price 5/- Net

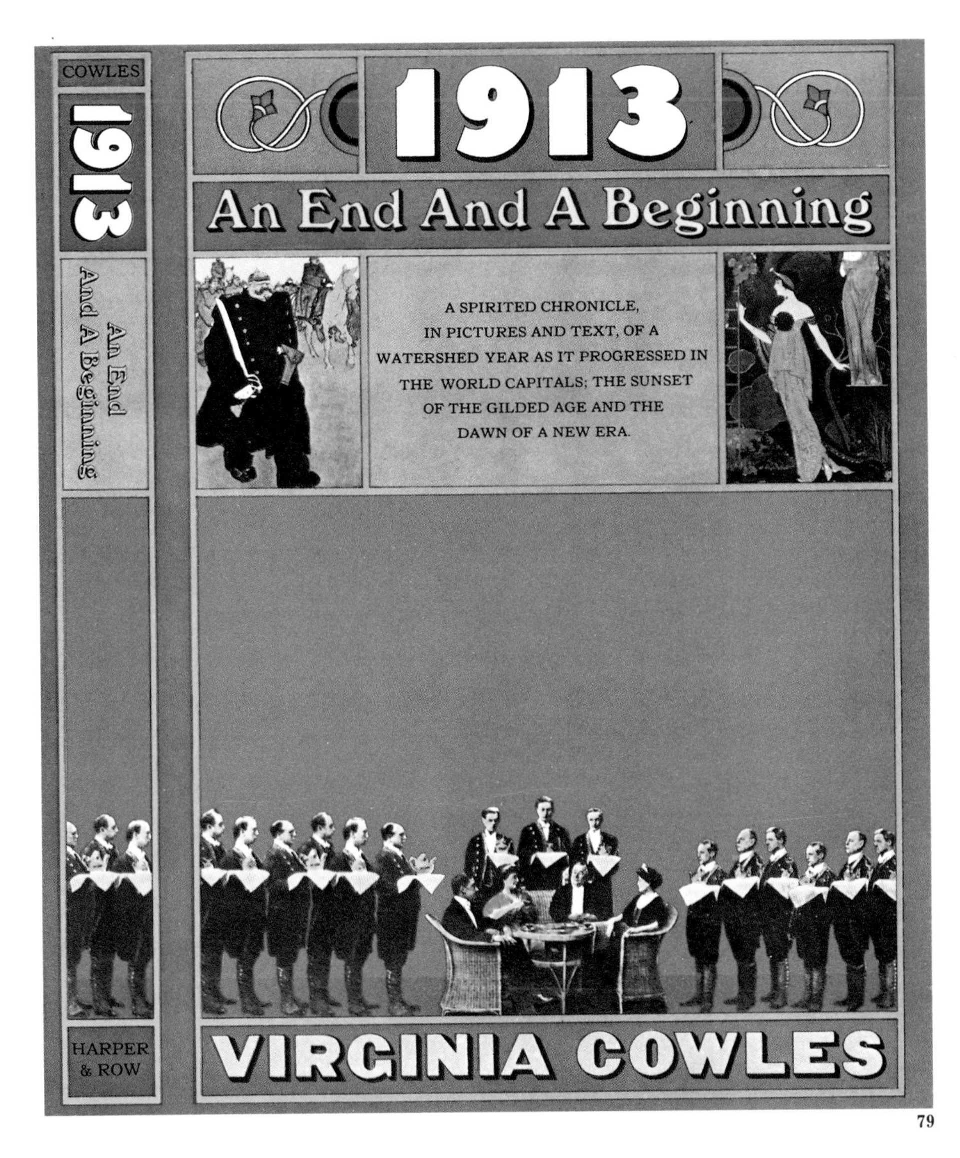

79

80

With most of the thousand-odd book jackets and paperback covers I've designed, my inclination has been to use a large image with small type. Hence, I've not done much work for mass market paperbacks or best-seller hardcover books, where large type is mandatory. My jacket for **[77]** *Our Crowd*, a book about the German-Jewish aristocracy in nineteenth-century America, was an exception to this rule. In spite of the non-best-seller type of cover, the book sold very well. **[78]** *Corvo*, a jacket for a book about a famous mystic, was inspired by Aubrey Beardsley's cover for *The Yellow Book*. Though stylistically different, the composition of Beardsley's drawing and his geometric design influenced a number of my jackets, including **[79]** *1913*, a history of that pre-war year. For this jacket, I took images from the book and reproduced them. For **[80]** I drew nearly identical twins. The duplication was deliberately jarring and mysterious.

[81-86] I designed numerous advertisements for printers, typographers, color separators, and others to appear in *Push Pin Graphic* in exchange for production services. While each fit into the design character of the *Graphic*, these ads like any other were intended to sell products and services effectively. Some of the ads were more interesting than the editorial matter.

81

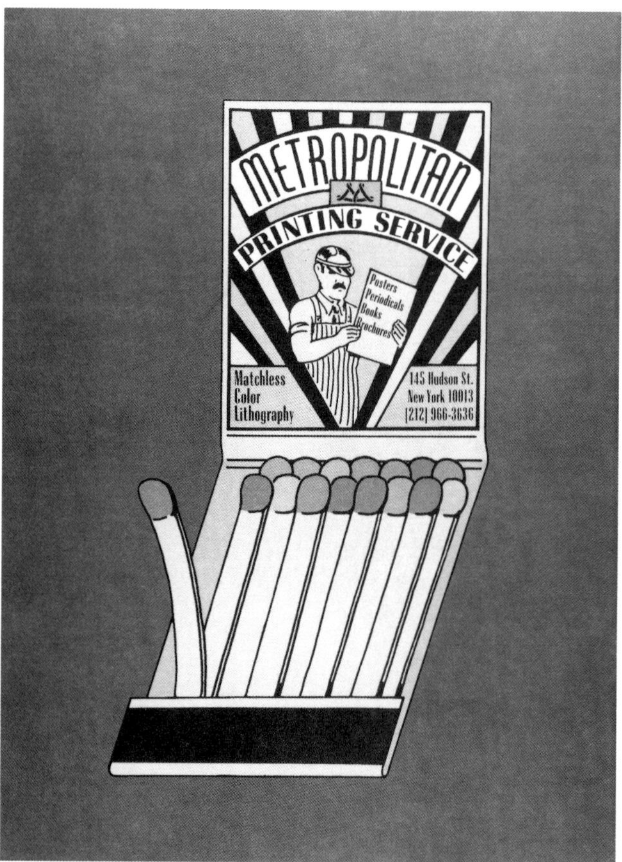

84

CHARLES TOOR INC.
228 E 45 ST N.Y. 10017 TEL (212) 687-5470
METAL AND FILM TYPOGRAPHY
TOOR TYPE
WE DELIVER

82

PIONEER-MOSS
"Stanley Tankel.
I'm in Graphic Reproduction.
Glad to meet you."
PIONEER-MOSS

83

Serving New York Since 1940
Metropolitan
Printing Service
145 Hudson Street, New York 10013, (212) 966-3636
Quality Color Lithography

85

METROPOLITAN
PRINTS BEAUTIFUL
GREENS
AND BLUES AND REDS AND SILVERS AND PURPLES AND BLACKS AND ORANGES
SALAD TURNIP
SPINACH
CELERY
CABBAGE
METROPOLITAN PRINTING SERVICE
QUALITY COLOR LITHOGRAPHY

86

[87-95] I began doing *Forbes* magazine advertising in 1978. The images were originally done as print ads and then enlarged to poster size. I usually render a drawing in black line and send it to a color process shop where my drawing is photomechanically reproduced on white plasticized paper. I then apply Cello-Tak color sheets to this print and cut out the color areas I want. If I'm not satisfied, color areas can be changed by peeling off the sheets. With the early ads, I was given a basic idea—to wed *Forbes* to sporting events. In the first series, the players were shown ahead of the pack, reading the magazine. In the recent series, the magazine is used symbolically as the object that gets the reader to the top.

87

88

89

90

91

92

93

Forbes helps you
set your
sights higher.
Forbes
Capitalist Tool®

94

Forbes
Capitalist Tool®

96

97

[96-98] Many of my recent assignments have been for computer companies or magazines. My approach is to humanize the machines. Two of these drawings of seemingly absurd (in fact they're not so farfetched) uses for the personal computer were originally done for an IBM calendar, which was rejected. The *Frankfurter Allgemeine Magazin* bought them as illustrations for a feature. They asked me to generate the additional bucolic scene below left.

98

[99] These monoprints were illustrations for poetry published in *Evergreen Review*. The accidents endemic to this technique helped me evoke feelings that I could not have otherwise achieved with other, more controlled methods.

[100] Portraits of Lester Flatt and Earl Scruggs were done for a keepsake on bluegrass music designed and hand-printed by Mo Lebowitz. The earthiness of the woodcut medium fit the subject.

99

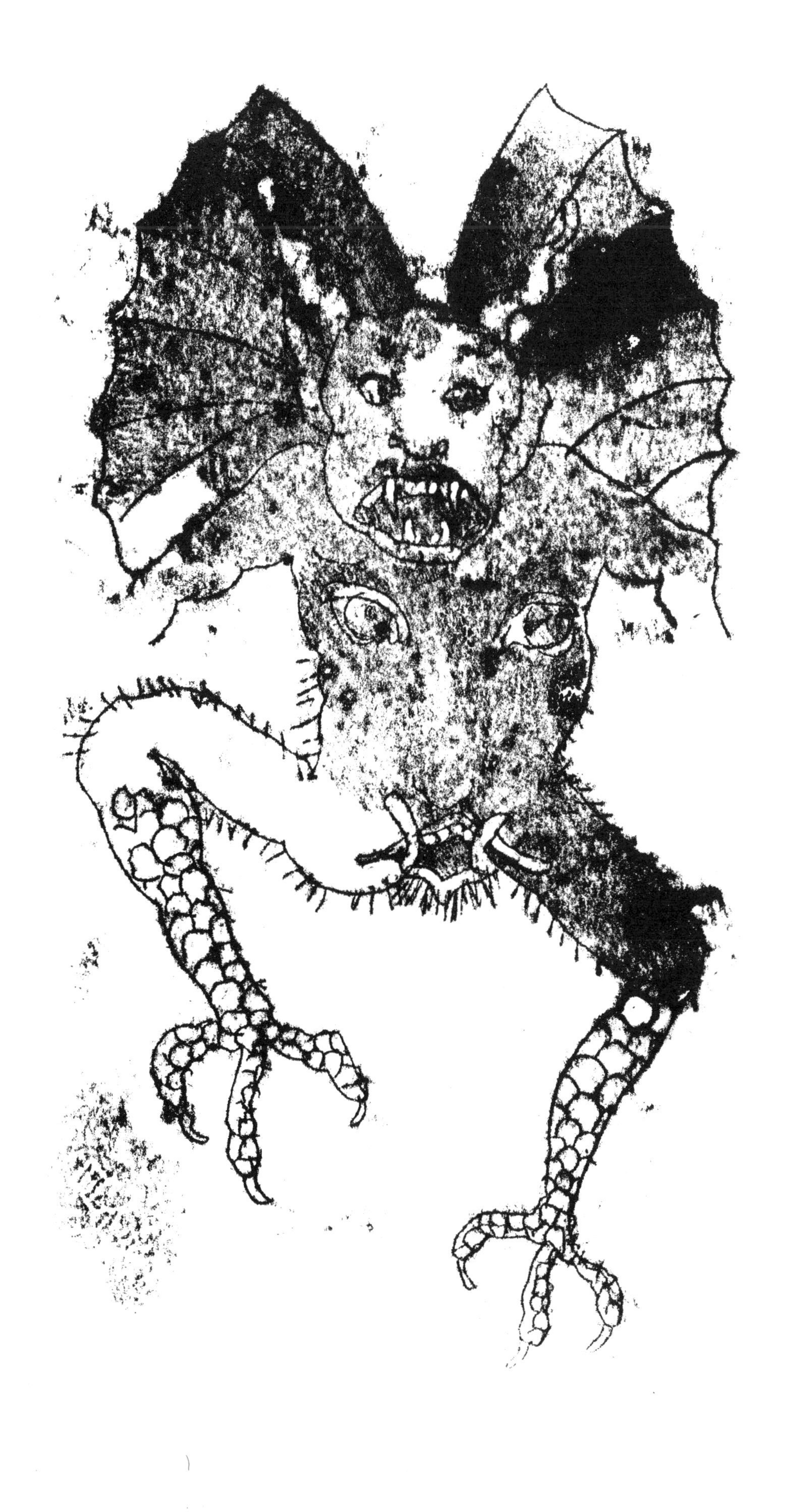

100

101

102

Consider these illustrations homage to my Eastern European heritage. [101] I did this painting for "When Schlemiel Went To Warsaw," a children's story by I.B. Singer published in *Audience* magazine, about a man who sets out to Warsaw from his little town. Stopping along the way to sleep, he points his boots in the direction of Warsaw so that he will correctly continue his travels the next day. That night some joker turns his boots around, so in the morning our hero walks in the direction whence he came. He arrives in what he thinks is Warsaw but is, in fact, the town he has left. He lives there happily ever after. For the painting I chose a primitive/surrealist approach [102] I did this ad to promote a German printing ink. The colorful, printed bird poster contrasts with the dreary environment.

The Age of Nixon 1969 to 197—
THE
FEBRUARY 1972
$1.00
Atlantic
MONTHLY
The Square Majority by Stewart Alsop
LBJ and the Kennedys by Michael Janeway

104

103

105

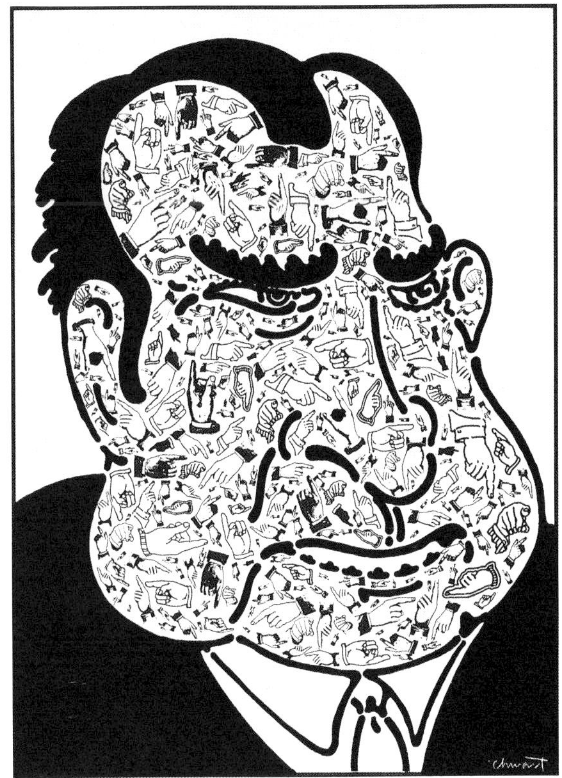
106

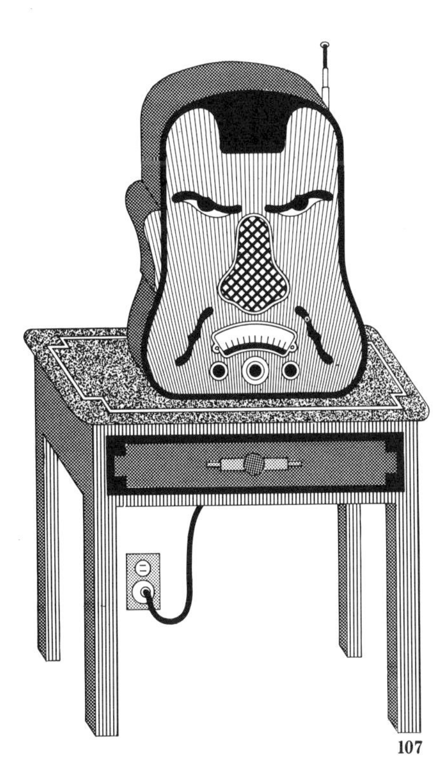
107

Some of my most satisfying drawings were executed during the Nixon presidency, and especially during the Watergate affair. Nixon was the caricaturist's dream and my favorite target. Even nature conspired against him —with that comic hooter and witch's peak hair line, his features needed only slight exaggeration. **[103]** In the mummy illustration for the Op-Ed Page of the *New York Times*—a combination of monoprint and crayon—very little of Nixon had to be exposed to render him recognizable. Often I was asked to illustrate articles written by Nixon's detractors. Being one myself was helpful in the problem solving. The idea for the drawings to accompany **[104]** "The Square Majority" for the *Atlantic*, and **[105]** "The Nixon Fortress" in the *New York Times Magazine* came literally from the titles, which simplified, through metaphor, the complex ideas of the pieces in the same way that my drawings did. The styles I employed in both cases were determined by the subject matter: a mechanically done schematic was best to show the conformity of Middle America and a medieval woodcut-like drawing was the best way to render a castle. **[106]** For the Op-Ed Page of the *New York Times*, all fingers pointed to the Guilty One, and **[107]** for "Nixon and the FCC," a story about the President's plan to control the media, Nixon metamorphosed into a radio. I drew a radio that echoed the thirties deco period because it had more human characteristics. **[108]** When Nixon retired, drawing cartoons of politicians was not much fun, until Ronald Reagan was elected.

108

[109-110] The *Frankfurter Allgemeine Magazin* has a striking design originated by the late Willy Fleckhaus. For a feature of my work, I was asked to do a self-portrait. Responding to my self-effacing nature, I made my nose into a clown's head and I reversed the idea for the opening illustration inside.

110

111

112

113

114

Anthropomorphism, giving human traits to animals, is one of the conceptual tools I occasionally use. In the examples here each animal embodies a different degree of symbolic significance. **[111]** Art for a 24-sheet billboard advertising a seafood restaurant in Houston. Their catch is flown in fresh daily. **[112]** For an article in the *New York Times Magazine* on self-testing for alcoholism, I used the monkey as a symbol because it is so often used for laboratory tests. I must, however, confess to some mockery here, since in this case the monkey is testing himself. **[113]** For a cover story in the *Boston Globe Magazine* on veterinary hospitals, the idea was not as important to me as the design elements. I like the way the cow's head plays off the spoked wheel. **[114]** *With A Song In My Art: The Musical Image* is a poster done for an exhibition of record cover art. Drawn with brush and ink, it was printed as a silk screen in dark blue and silver, on wrapping paper. The talented monkey comes from a bit of carnival ephemera; the pipe is my own.

[115-116] I made two treks to 42nd Street in order to do drawings of porn parlors. I've always been a voyeur, but the idea came to me because I wanted to work in the style of Indian miniatures. The pornographic setting was similar to that in some of those pictures, because the strippers performed on a runway similar to the raised terraces in formal Indian images. The first image, an acrylic painting of a peep show, was done for myself. The second, of a live sex show, done in pen-and-ink with Cello-Tak, was for a story in the *Frankfurter Allgemeine Magazin.* I was too embarrassed to make on-the-spot sketches, so both were from memory.

CHWAST

[117] My favorite poster is *My Best Work*. The concept was inspired by the Belgian woodcut novelist Frans Masereel. The style derived from a comic strip in *Jugend*, a German satire magazine. Many of Masereel's books focused on an elusive muse who drives the artist-protagonist to despair. While my character is not desperate, he is decidedly obsessed.

[118] Here is an illustration for a piece in *Esquire* on the problems of being short; a sensitive issue, exacerbated at the time by Randy Newman's musical attack, the song called "Short People." Though I'm of average height, my sympathy is always with the oppressed, and Toulouse-Lautrec is decidedly oppressed in this situation. While the symbolism will not go over anyone's head, there is a second level of meaning: these are boring people, who think they're big, and who are ignoring a great artist because of his height. Lautrec is shown as so small that he has to drink from a shot glass.

Paper: Mead Terra Text 70 lb.

A Retrospective Exhibition of Design, Illustration and Photography Selected by the Artists

John Alcorn
Ted Andresakes
Sam Antupit
Emil Antonucci
Dominic Arbitrio
Herman Aronson
R. O. Blechman
Bruce Blackburn
Arthur Boden
Ewald Breuer
Bruno Brugnatelli
Will Burtin
Jesse Califano
Vincent Ceci
Ivan Chermayeff
Roger Cook
Al Corchia
Seymour Chwast
Richard Danne
Paul Davis
Rudolph de Harak
Joseph del Gaudio
Joseph Bourke Del Valle
Seldon Dix
Lou Dorfsman
Bill Duevell
David Enock
Sandy Erickson
Ed Fitt
Beau Gardner
Thomas Geismar
John Gilbert
Milton Glaser
Diana Graham
Norman Green
Norman Griner
Robert Grossman
Richard Henderson
Dick Hess
Clyde Hogg
Harry Jacobs
Hedda Johnson
Art Kane
Mo Lebowitz
George Lois
Herb Lubalin
Giuseppe Lucci
Jay Maisel
Mary Matthews
Peter Max
James Mc Mullan
James Miho
Tomoko Miho
John Milligan
Ron Morgan
Luanne Mount
Jon Naar
David November
Robert Paganucci
Don Page
Tony Palladino
Jim Pringle
Paul Rand
Jack Reich
Kenneth Resen
Doyle Robinson
Arnold Saks
Robert Salpeter
Cosmos Sarchiapone
Sheldon Seidler
Isadore Seltzer
Gene Sercander
Don Shanosky
Amasa G. Smith, Jr.
Edward Sorel
William Tobias
Don Trousdell
George Tscherny
Massimo Vignelli
Barry Zaid
Roger Zimmerman

March 17 to April 30, 1971
Monday through Friday
9 am to 5 pm

Mead Library of Ideas
Pan Am Building
200 Park Avenue,
New York, N.Y.
(212) 972-2347

117

„So—o. Denn kannſt woll den Sack da mitnehmen."

118

119

120

[119] This illustration was for a short story in *Audience* in which a young executive has a tryst at a motel with his new secretary. She does not come to the office the next morning, but leaves a note instead. It states that the activities of the previous night were photographed, and that they will be made public unless he renews his subscription to *Newsweek*. (A photographer is peeking through the crack in the venetian blinds.)

[120] This was an illustration for a story called "Overcoat II," a somewhat updated, yet skewed sequel to Gogol's *The Overcoat*, about a petty clerk who, after suffering the cold for many years, acquires a coat. In the new version, the fellow gets his much-needed apparel, but it is eventually confiscated by the authorities because he bought it on the black market. In this scene, he is trying on the precious object for the first time.

121

[121] For a record album cover of *The Threepenny Opera*, I approximated the look of a woodcut in the style of German Expressionist art. Based on John Gay's original, *The Threepenny Opera* is set in England in the 1890s, but the German relationship—through Weill and Brecht, of course—is so strong that I inevitably drew upon a German graphic influence.

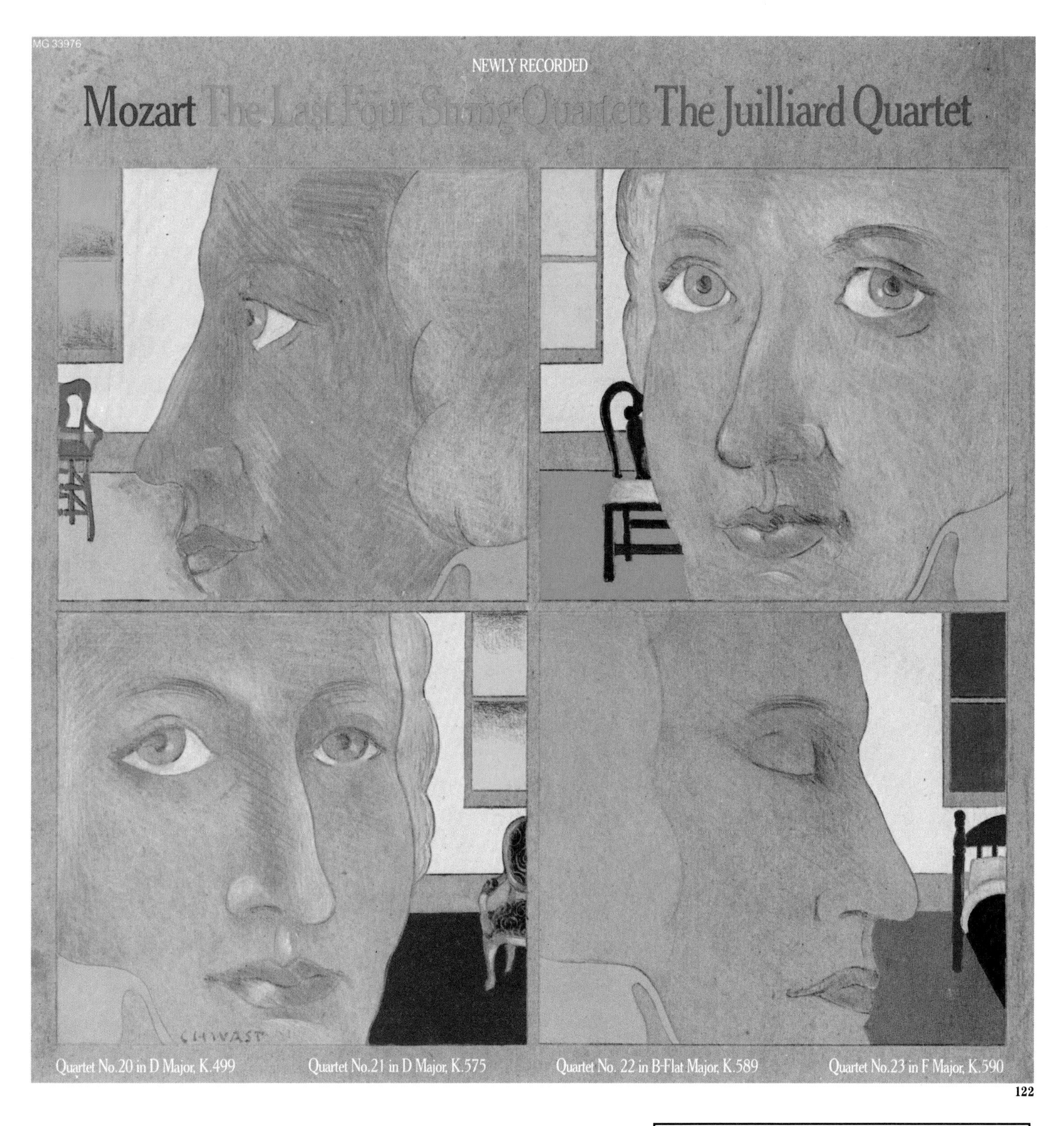

122

[122] There is no special theme that binds Mozart's last four string quartets together. Therefore, the only elements I had to work with for this recording were Mozart and the number four. My solution was to do a sequence showing Mozart in four stages of his life. However, rather than radically change the portrait, I showed in the background a high chair, a desk chair, an easy chair, and, finally, a bed to symbolize the stages. The light outside the window reinforces the notion.

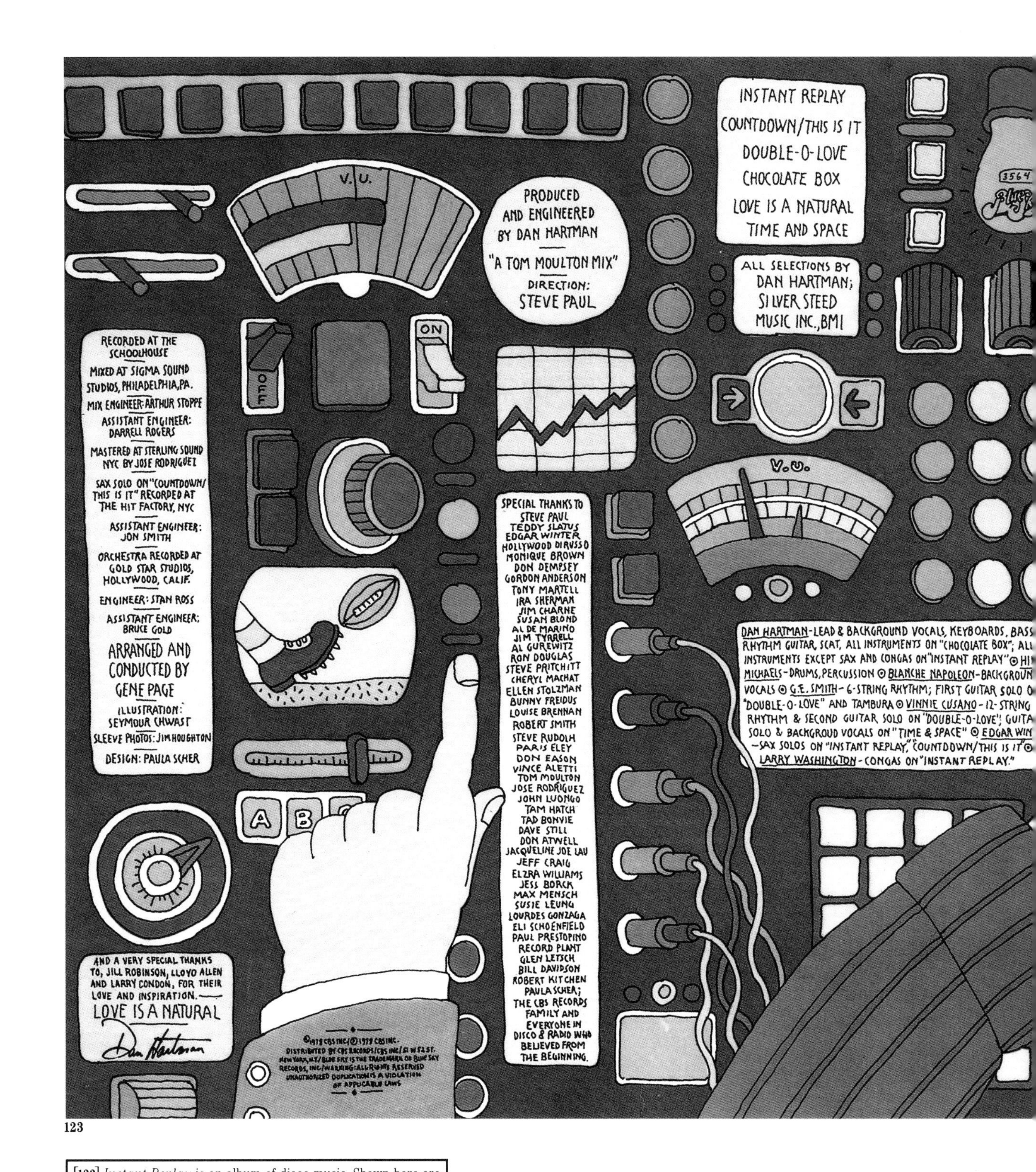

123

[**123**] *Instant Replay* is an album of disco music. Shown here are the front and back covers. The art director asked me to do a crazy machine to represent a synthesizer. Because the drawing was so intricate, I was forced to render all the cover and liner notes lettering by hand because typography would have fought with the art.

[124] This illustration for the front and back of a record album is for one of a series CBS produced, called "Rock-and-Roll Revolution." It was inspired by an R. Taylor cartoon that I saw in *The New Yorker* when I was a child. In the original, marching groups of angry striking workers are about to converge at a corner.

MONTREUX SUMMIT
VOLUME 2
BOB JAMES · GEORGE DUKE · BILLY COBHAM · RALPH MACDONALD · STEVE KHAN · JANNE SCHAFFER · ERIC GALE · STAN GETZ · WOODY SHAW
ALPHONSO JOHNSON · DEXTER GORDON · BENNY GOLSON · HUBERT LAWS · BOBBI HUMPHREY · THIJS VAN LEER · MAYNARD FERGUSON

125

ILEANA COTRUBAS
PLACIDO DOMINGO
IN
DONIZETTI:
L'ELISIR D'AMORE
SIR GERAINT EVANS
INGVAR WIXELL
LILLIAN WATSON
ORCHESTRA AND CHORUS
OF THE ROYAL OPERA HOUSE
COVENT GARDEN
JOHN PRITCHARD
CONDUCTOR

126

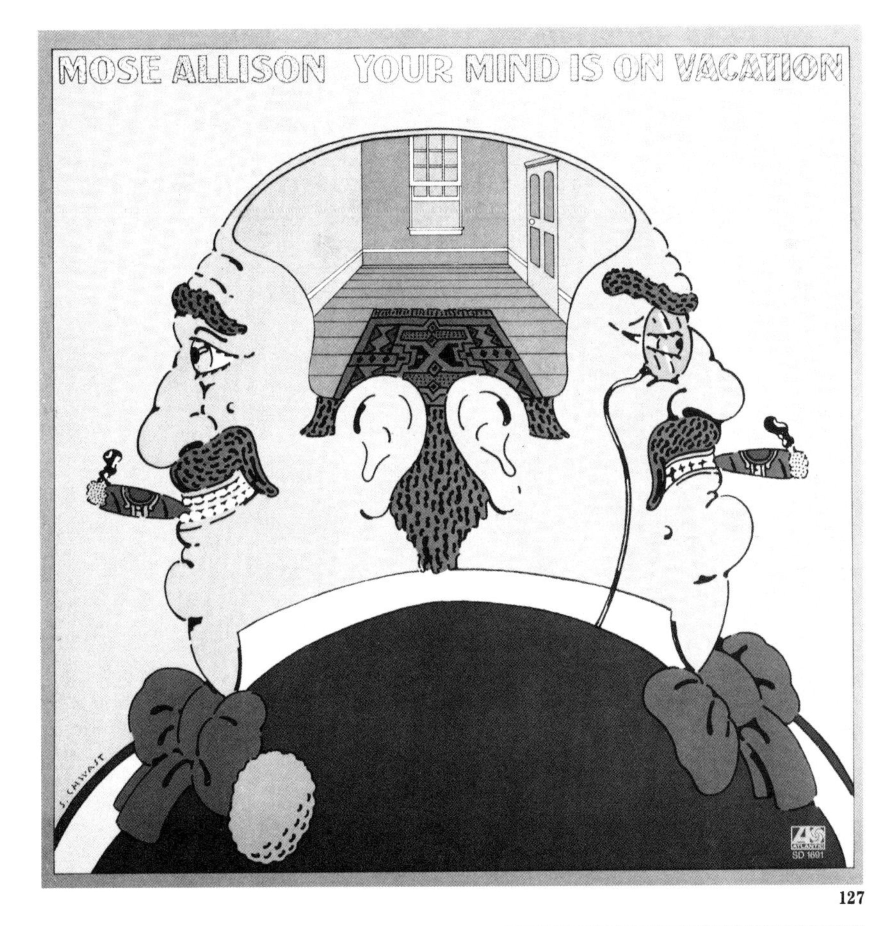

127

128

[125] *Montreux Summit,* rendered in colored pencil, was a nice idea, but required a lot more patience than I had at the time.

[126] Columbia Records commissioned this sketch, ultimately rejected, for Donizetti's "L'Elisir d'Amore." The idea came from Catholic votive paintings, usually painted in oil on tin, and always including a heavenly vision. Illustrated is a nineteenth-century Italian example.

[127] For *Mose Allison Your Mind Is On Vacation,* the art director asked me to draw a double head with a vacant room in the brain. He told Allison that I was going to do an anatomical drawing. Mose was surprised when he saw the finish, because he was expecting an *atomical* drawing. He liked it anyway.

[128] *Stephane Grappelli* is a jazz violinist whose work is played in discos. As I am known as a shoe fetishist, the art director permitted me to satisfy my own desires.

Story by Phyllis La Farge
Pictures by Seymour Chwast
THE PANCAKE KING

Henry was rich now (and so was Mr. Jinker). He had given Mother and Father a pearl-gray Buick with red fox upholstery. He didn't see them much any more. He had a white Buick (to match his suit). Mr. Jinker drove and Henry sat in back. Ezra sat beside Henry in a special basket lined with a plaid steamer rug.
One day just as they were about to set out in the white Buick to visit a few of the forty-three restaurants of the Pancake King chain, which they inspected in person every week, the White House called to ask whether Henry could get there in time for brunch. There were some Chinese ambassadors coming . . . they wanted to serve them something really American . . . they would send a plane. . . .
Henry got there.
129

I've written and/or illustrated over a dozen children's books. My only prerequisite is that they be fanciful or mysterious. Straight storytelling does not interest or challenge me. **[129]** *The Pancake King* is a story about a little boy who becomes world famous for making the best pancakes. In this picture, his agent is driving him to the White House. The entire book was drawn in outline; color areas were marked and colors indicated by sketches from which the printer then prepared color plates. This is the most effective way to print flat art.

The Flip-Flap
Limerickricks
Designed and
Illustrated
by Seymour Chwast
A Push Pin Book
Random House

There was a young man named Paul
Who went to a fancy dress ball;
He thought he would risk it
And go as a biscuit—
But a dog ate him up in the hall!

There was a young man named Paul
Who went to a fancy dress ball;
He thought he would risk it
And go as a biscuit—
But a dog ate him up in the hall!

130

131

Here are two books that involve manipulation. **[130]** In *Limerick-ricks* an object in the illustration is completely transformed by unfolding the page. The punchline of the limerick is revealed by the reader's action. **[131]** A new element is added to each verse in the branching poem, *The House That Jack Built.* I designed a book that would grow as the verses were read and the pages were turned. As the poem gets longer, the pages get larger, the type size increases, and more images are added to the composition.

132

[132] In *Tall City, Wide Country,* a book that reads frontwards and backwards, it is necessary to turn the book ninety degrees in the middle to continue the story, no matter which way you are going.

[133] Etienne D'Elessert asked me to illustrate an unexpurgated version of "Bushy Bridge," a Norwegian story, for a series he produced of classic fairy tales. Before it had been bowdlerized, the original required the heroine to kiss some rather grotesque characters (shown here). The drawings were done on chipboard with colored pencil and acrylic.

133

And then

Through the wide country

A snake slithers

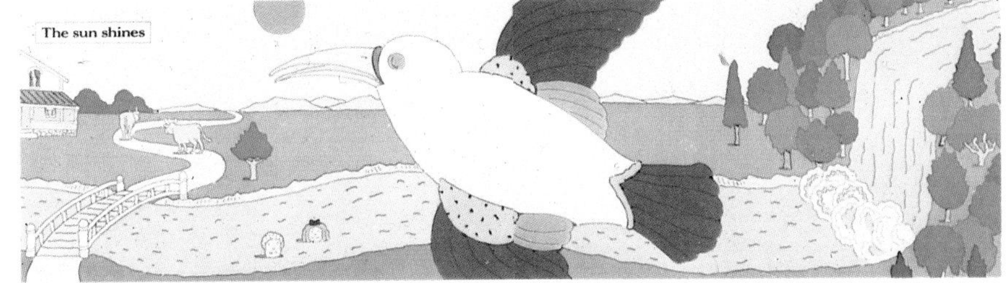
The sun shines

Cows moo

In the wide country

Tall City, Wide Country
A Book to Read Forward and Backward
By Seymour Chwast

134

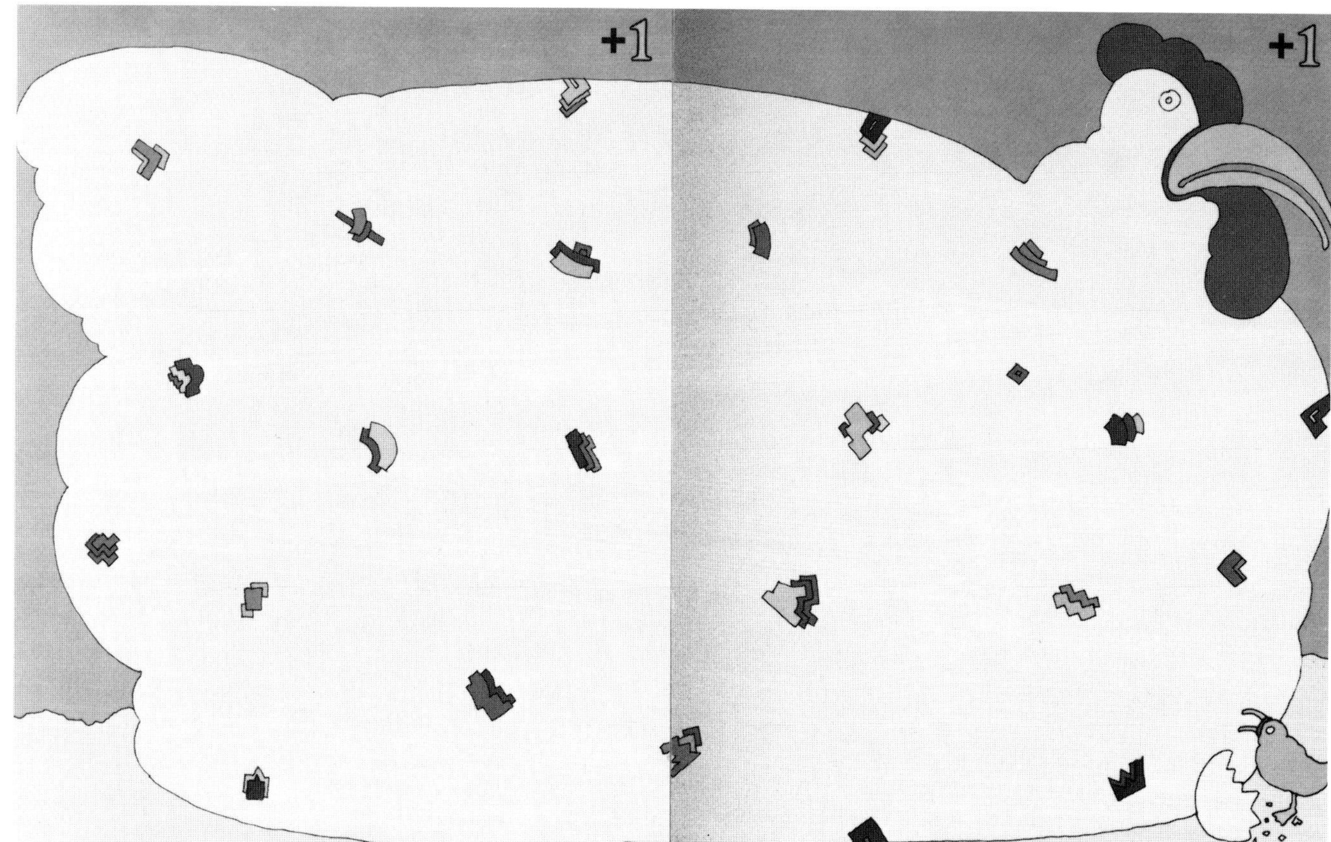

135

[134-136] I collaborated with Martin Moskof on *Still Another Alphabet Book, Still Another Numbers Book,* and *Still Another Children's Book.* They were our renditions of the most common forms of children's books.

136

NUMBER ONE

THE PUSH PIN Monthly Graphic. MARCH 1957

Published by The Push Pin Studios, 211 East 57 Street, New York 22, PLaza 3 5616 — Designers & Illustrators to Advertising & Industry — Miss Rosalie Janpol, representative.

Devil's Apple.

(Solanum mammosum L.)

137

138

139

The *Push Pin Almanack* was started in 1953 by Ed Sorel, Reynold Ruffins, and myself, as a promotion piece. After the forming of Push Pin Studios, we decided that the almanac format was too confining and, thus, went to the other extreme with a large format broadside. In 1957, the *Monthly Graphic* began. Included were articles, reprints of fiction, and a variety of other excuses to show off our illustration and design. Each issue was based on a different theme. Sometimes it was a showcase for one of us; at other times we collaborated. **[137]** For the first issue of the *Monthly Graphic,* I did a woodcut of an odd plant called the Devil's Apple. **[138-139]** In one issue, devoted to the thirties, I illustrated a flapper and a meeting in which Mussolini planned his rise to power—both also in woodcut.

Roscoe (Fatty)
Arbuckle
Typical of many of the popular comics in the early 1900's, "Fatty" Arbuckle was also larger and more colorful than life. His obesity, which amounted to 350 pounds, made his extreme agility and dexterity hilariously funny. He was an appealing innocent, always running into misfortune but winning the heroine in the end. The various roles he portrayed, such as the Keystone cop, the bumbling country boy, and the balloon sized lady, were considered the essence of good clean Mack Sennett slapstick and brought great joy to millions of Americans.

140

[140] This is a spread from the "Good And Evil" issue of the *Push Pin Graphic.* Fatty Arbuckle fit the bill: on the good side, he was one of America's leading silent film comedians; and on the bad, he was accused and brought to trial for the murder of a showgirl. He was eventually acquitted, but his career was nonetheless ruined. I did this as a color linoleum cut.

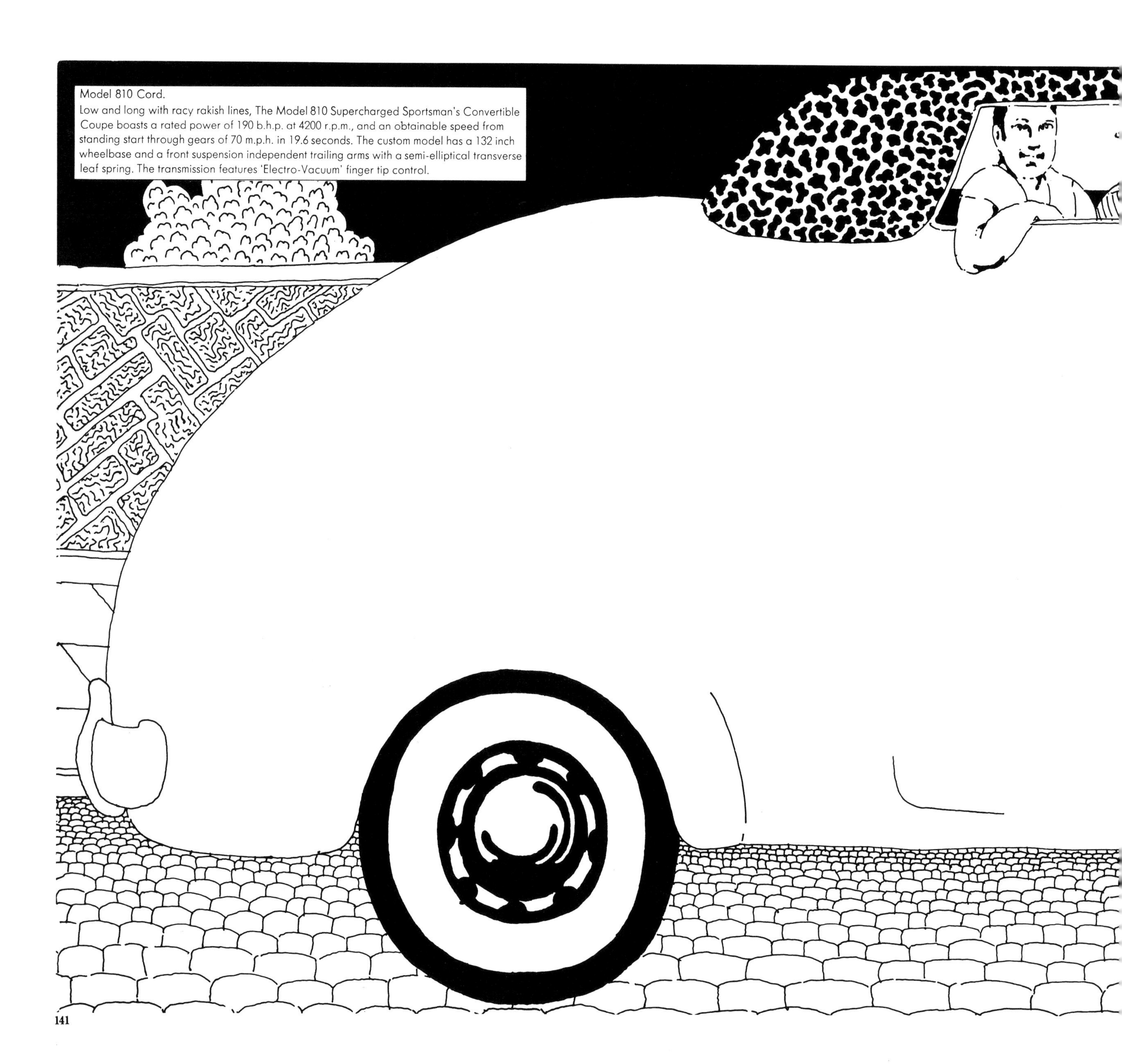

Model 810 Cord.
Low and long with racy rakish lines, The Model 810 Supercharged Sportsman's Convertible Coupe boasts a rated power of 190 b.h.p. at 4200 r.p.m., and an obtainable speed from standing start through gears of 70 m.p.h. in 19.6 seconds. The custom model has a 132 inch wheelbase and a front suspension independent trailing arms with a semi-elliptical transverse leaf spring. The transmission features 'Electro-Vacuum' finger tip control.

[141] This was an illustration for the "Classic Car Issue" of the *Push Pin Graphic.* Because of the large, flat area of the automobile the tension occurs on the outside of the drawing, rather than in the central image.

[142] This issue of the *Push Pin Graphic* was done in 1969 as a response to a period of civil rights activism in the south. My idea in designing this was to contrast popular images of Dixie with current events. Each color piece represented the old, and was rendered in a different style in order to approximate the look of the found pieces of art I borrowed from. A black-and-white newspicture showing the current reality was imposed over each mythic image and a bullet hole was die-cut through every page. The photographs showed Mrs. Viola Liuzzo, housewife, shot to death for giving a ride to civil rights workers; Emmitt Till, age 15, shot for allegedly whistling at a white girl; Harry Moore, leader of the Florida NAACP, killed by a bomb blast; Medgar Evers, civil rights leader, murdered by a sniper; Goodman, Chaney, and Schwerner, activists, beaten and killed; Martin Luther King, Jr., assassinated. With the final image of the March on Washington, the situation was reversed; the news photograph was blown to full page and inset was an old Southern dame shot through the head, signifying the emergence of a new consciousness.

The S●uth

142

MRS. VIOLA GREGG LIUZZO 1927-1965
Selma, Alabama

Mrs. Viola Liuzzo, 38 year old white housewife and mother of five, was shot to death while returning to Montgomery from Selma, where she had delivered a carload of civil rights workers who took part in the Freedom march. Mrs. Liuzzo was shot through the head by a high-powered rifle by unidentified men in another car.

Rose Of Alabama

Oh! lovely Rose! The Rose of Alabama,
The sweetest flower earth knows
Is the Rose of Alabama.

One pleasant balmy night in June
When swung in silvery floods, the moon
My heart awoke love's vesper tune
For Rose of Alabama.

Then shrine-like, in my native land
Love's Eden! — shall my cottage stand
With happiness on every hand!
Sweet Rose of Alabama.

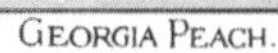
GEORGIA PEACH.

[143] The "Chicken" issue was everything you never knew you had to know about chickens. After this issue of the *Push Pin Graphic,* we ceased its informal format and it became a magazine.

[144] The line drawing of the Teutonic gourmands illustrated an article entitled "Why Germany Went To War," in our "Complete History and Knowledge of the World Condensed" issue. (Readers were told that the Germans made war because they were full of gas and had no southern outlet.)

[145] In "The Machine" issue our point of view was that old machines were more beautiful and functionally expressive than their contemporary, box-like, high-tech counterparts. I illustrated the death of the old-style machine by placing it in an electric chair.

NUMBER 63 Push Pin Graphic CHICKEN ISSUE

©1976 The Push Pin Studios, Inc. 207 East 32 Street New York 10016 Subscription: $6.00 six issues Outside U.S.: $7.50

CHICKEN!

A NOTE FROM THE EDITOR: WHY CHICKEN?

The general public for generations has had a misguided and somewhat demeaning attitude toward the importance of the chicken to the civilization of man.

The chicken has constantly been regarded as an unattractive, noisy, smelly bird that exists on a diet of low quality food; happily lays eggs, and is delicious broiled, boiled, fried, baked and poached. All this, of course, is true, but this tabloid serves to point out the long buried historic facts about the chicken and man, and why we are in continual debt to this magnificent bird.

THE CHICKEN IN HISTORY

BY POLLO SCHER

THE PREHISTORIC CHICKEN

TO answer the age old question of which came first, the chicken or the egg, the chicken came first. Its predecessor was the giant logundo bird which is still known to North-Eastern parts of outer Mongolia. It is believed that the giant logundo bird mated with the now extinct cockasouras and the result was chicken. The first known chicken is believed to have been sighted in what is now Red China, seven miles east of present day Peking. Archeologists have constructed a model of this prehistoric chicken, which is presently on display at the Museum of Natural History in St. Paul, Minnesota. The construction shows the bird to be approximately 6 feet 5 inches in height (from crown to claw) and the estimated weight of the bird is 247 lbs. Unfortunately, the left wing section is an imaginary construction, as the original bones are thought to be destroyed in an earthquake. The estimated date of this original chicken is 2,542 B.C.

THE CHINESE CHICKEN

OUR word "chicken" is derived from the Chinese "chi-ki-en" meaning large, ugly bird. It was later shortened to "chi-ken" which means ugly bird. According to Dr. Loa Su Sing, Chinese professor of archeology at Colum-

143

144

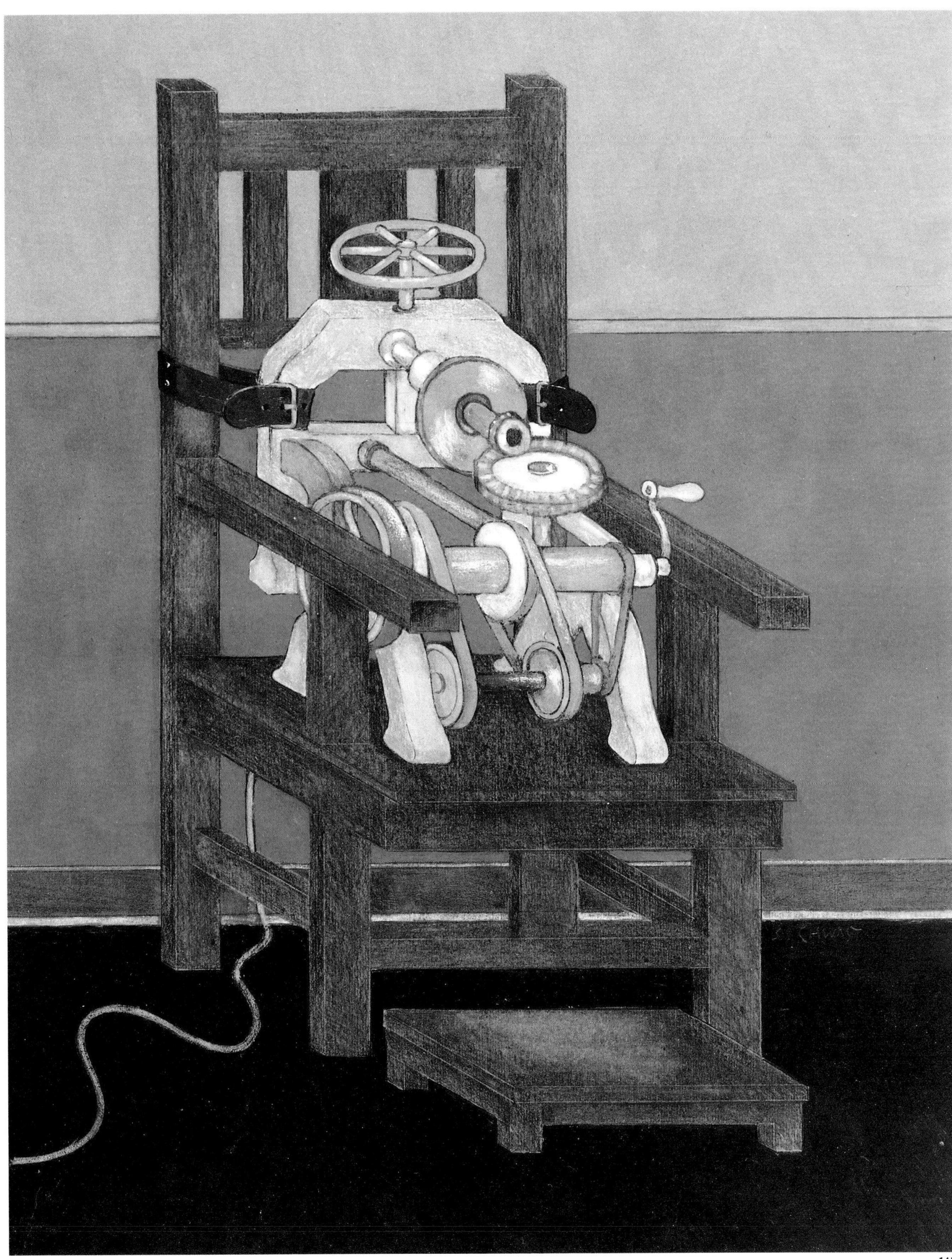

145

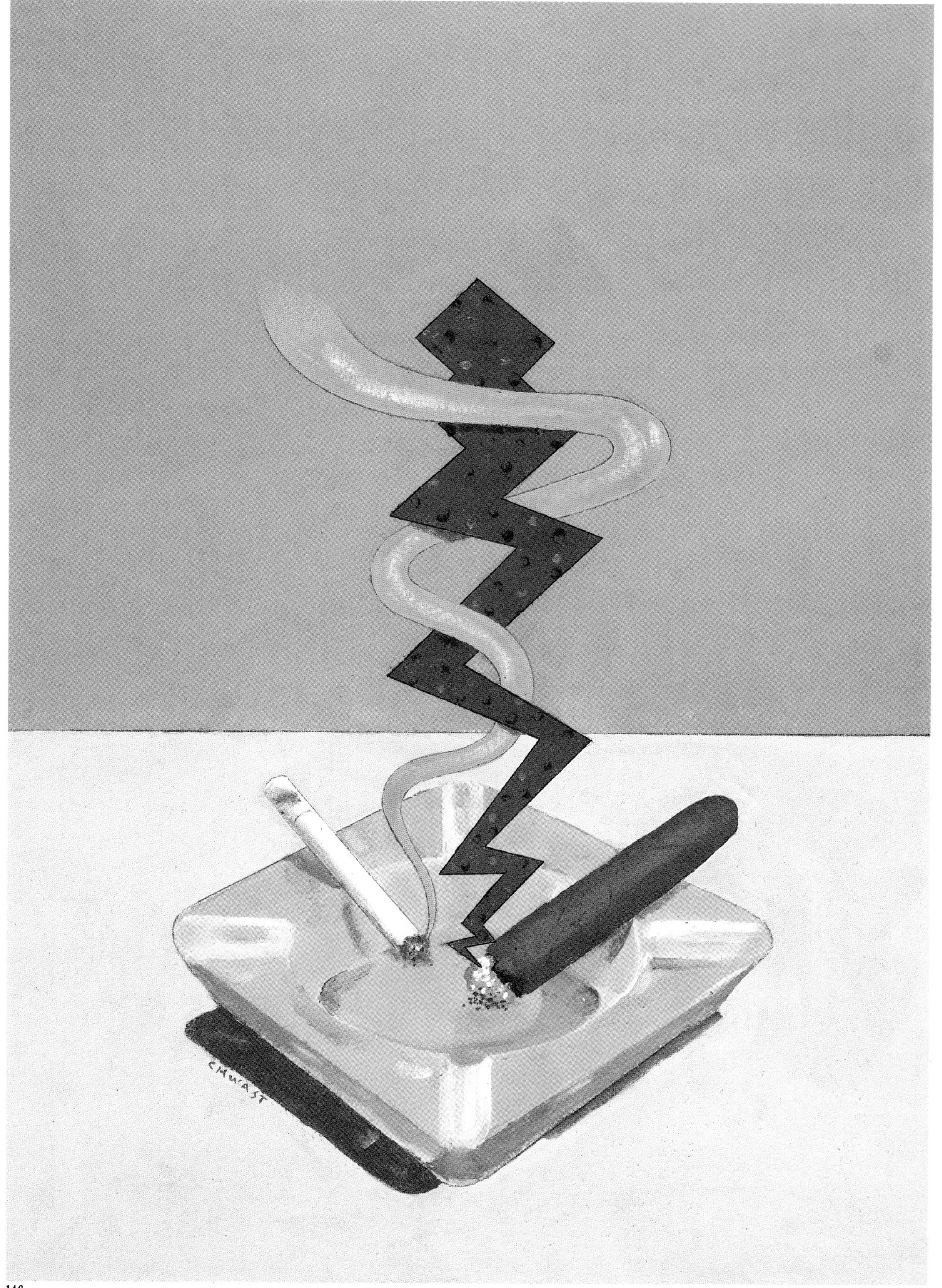

146

[146] For the cover of the "Couples" issue of the *Push Pin Graphic* I symbolized the relationship between a man and woman. **[147]** The impulse for "Coitus Topographicus," in the same issue, came from perusing a topographical map and an old sex manual I found in a second-hand bookstore. The idea just came together.

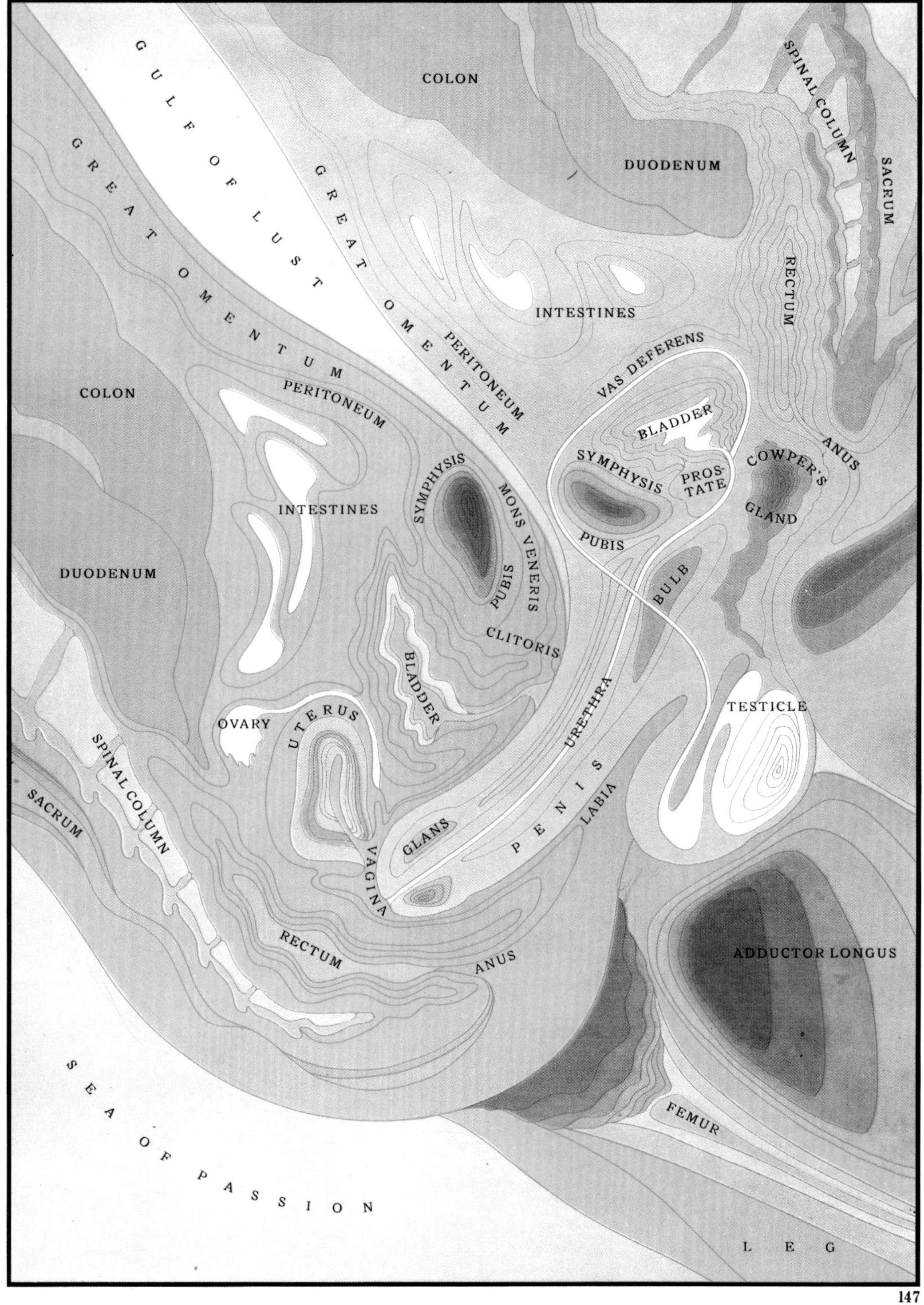

147

[148] Also in "The Complete History and Knowledge of the World Condensed" issue, I designed the "Push Pin Giant Pull Out 1977 Calendar Condensed," using pickup art in the date boxes. Shown here is half the year.

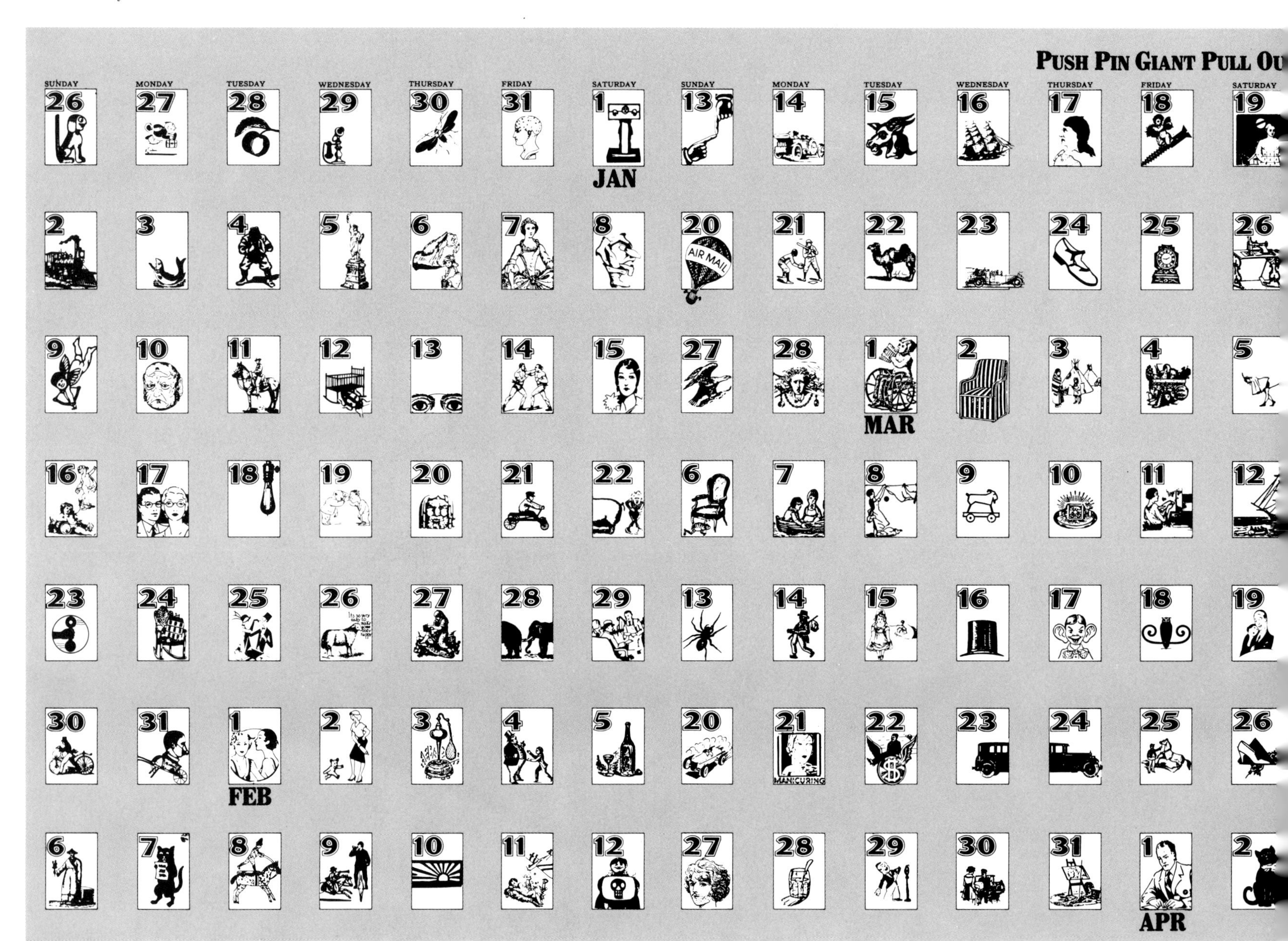

148

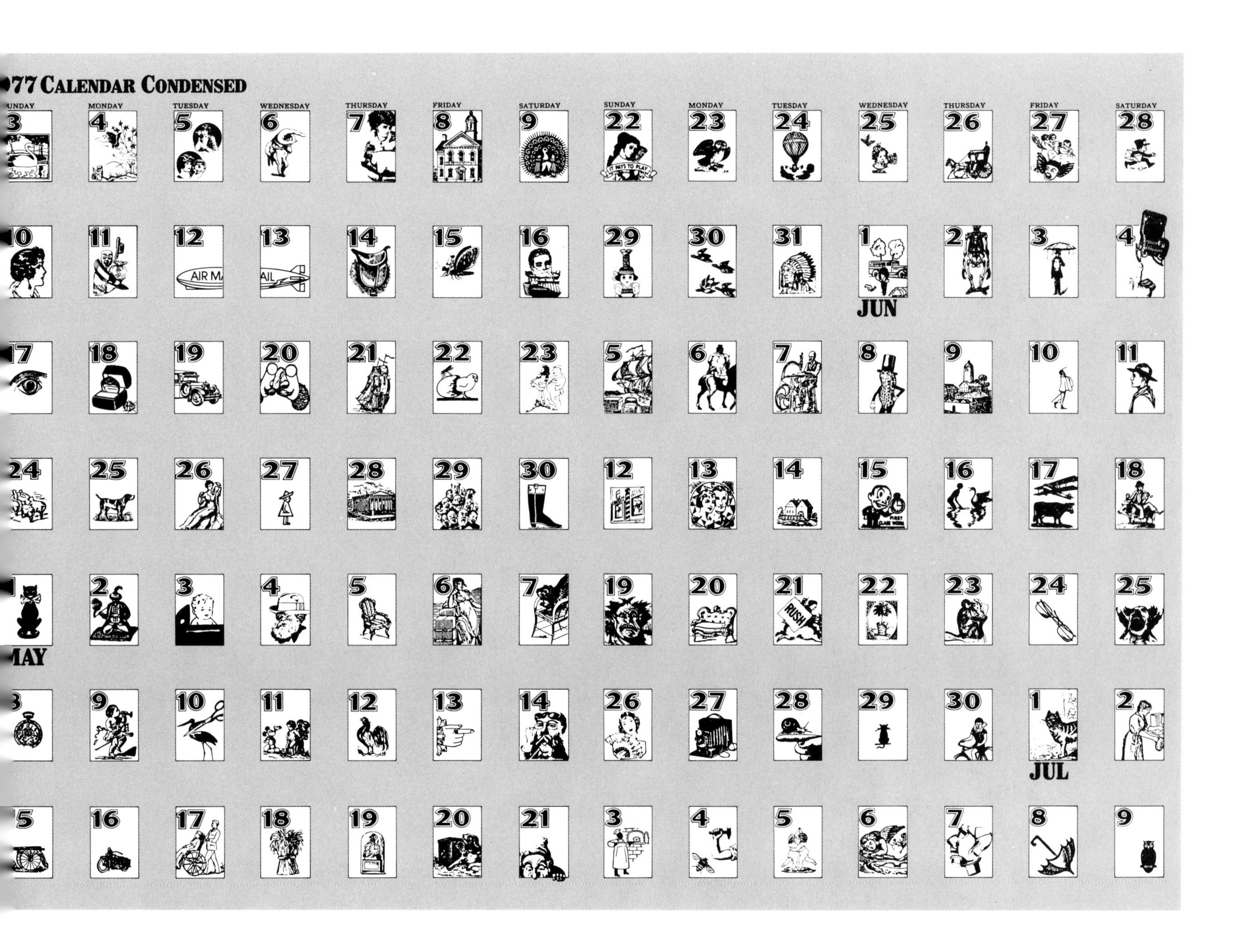

977 CALENDAR CONDENSED
SUNDAY
MONDAY
TUESDAY
WEDNESDAY
THURSDAY
FRIDAY
SATURDAY
SUNDAY
MONDAY
TUESDAY
WEDNESDAY
THURSDAY
FRIDAY
SATURDAY
3 4 5 6 7 8 9 22 23 24 25 26 27 28
IT PAYS TO PLAY
10 11 12 13 14 15 16 29 30 31 1 2 3 4
AIR MA
AIL
JUN
17 18 19 20 21 22 23 5 6 7 8 9 10 11
24 25 26 27 28 29 30 12 13 14 15 16 17 18
FIRST CLASS WORK
1 2 3 4 5 6 7 19 20 21 22 23 24 25
RUSH
MAY
8 9 10 11 12 13 14 26 27 28 29 30 1 2
JUL
15 16 17 18 19 20 21 3 4 5 6 7 8 9

Number 64 December 1976

♥ *Mothers.* ♥

150

[149-150] My favorite *Push Pin Graphic* was our "Mothers" issue. It was also the first issue using magazine format, and the first time a magazine had devoted itself to such an important subject. I illustrated the cover and did a portrait of the Cubist painter Juan Gris's mom. Other Push Pin illustrators portrayed the mothers of other famous artists, such as Toulouse-Lautrec, Giotto, and Jackson Pollock.

The Rest

[151] "The Great Frost," a fifteen-minute animated version of an episode in Virginia Woolf's novel *Orlando*, is one of six animated short films by different artists. The hour-long Christmas special for public television called *Simple Gifts* was produced and directed by R.O. Blechman. Fantasy and spectacle abound in this bittersweet tale. I provided the storyboard, background art, and model drawings for the animators who made the characters move. While my sensibilities are rooted in print, the added dimension of time that film provides offered additional creative possibilities.

151

While I've never designed a typeface for text, I've created a few headline alphabets, some of which began as hand lettering for posters. **[152]** This alphabet, called "Monograph," consists of 37 individually designed characters. I forgot to design a zero. **[153]** The "a" in "Artone" was originally designed as a trademark for an india ink (see page 41). I developed the rest of the alphabet because I liked the letter form, which is based on Art Nouveau. My fat, rounded alphabet is called "Blimp" for obvious reasons. Based on an old woodtype, it comes in three versions: solid, outline, and gradated. "Filmsense" was designed as a logo for a film division of Push Pin, and based on a letterhead that Milton Glaser did for the studio. "Myopic" was first used on a poster for *Mademoiselle*. The idea for the alphabet was that there could be an infinite number of drop-shadows and the designer could cut off whatever was unnecessary. "Buffalo" was commissioned by Mergenthaler Linotype. It was originally designed as a logo for "Buffalo Gum," a French product that was never produced.

152

153

[154] "Beastial Bold" originally ran in "The Not Quite Human" issue of the *Push Pin Graphic.* **[155]** "Alphabach" appeared in my book *Happy Birthday, Bach.*

154

155

GEORGE'S CAR WASH
1.50 MON.-FRI
HOT WAX 1.00
DRIVE IN
GLO WAX
OPEN 7 AM TO MID-NITE
VANS
PANELS
TRUCKS
2.50

156

The images on these pages are limited edition serigraphs. **[156]** *George's Car Wash* was originally done as an illustration in the "Travel to New Jersey" issue of the *Push Pin Graphic*. It is a well-known landmark and tourist attraction in the Garden State. **[157-158]** *With Remy* and *Still Life With Mack Truck* are both serigraphs. The former is a romantic image, the latter parodies still-life painting.

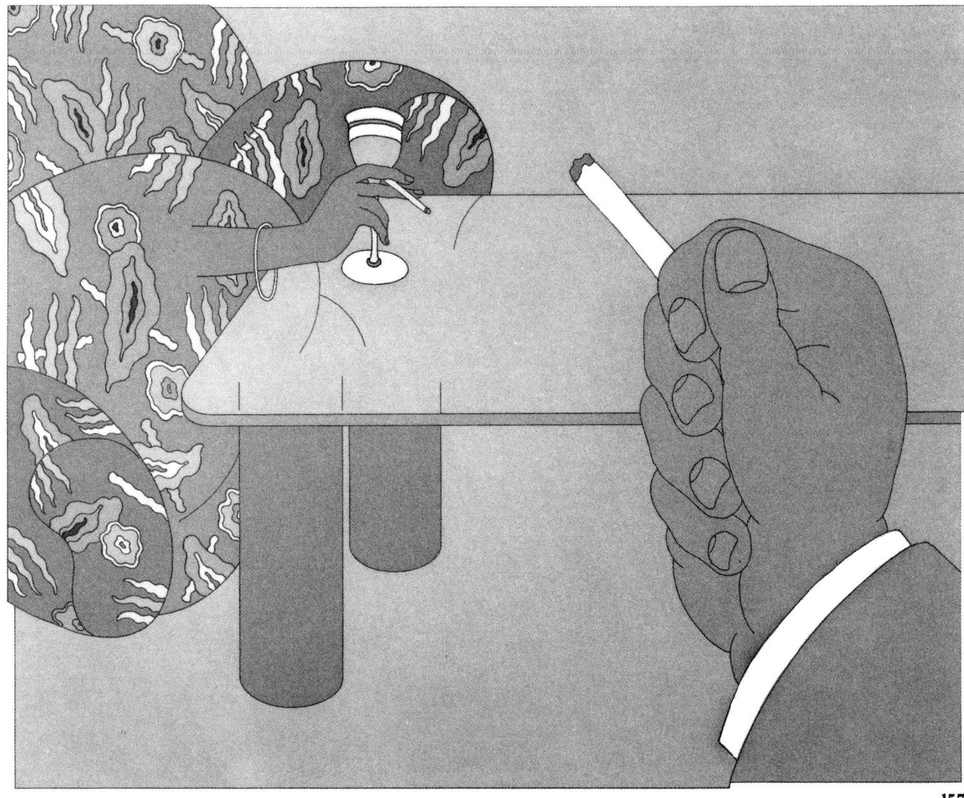

157

158

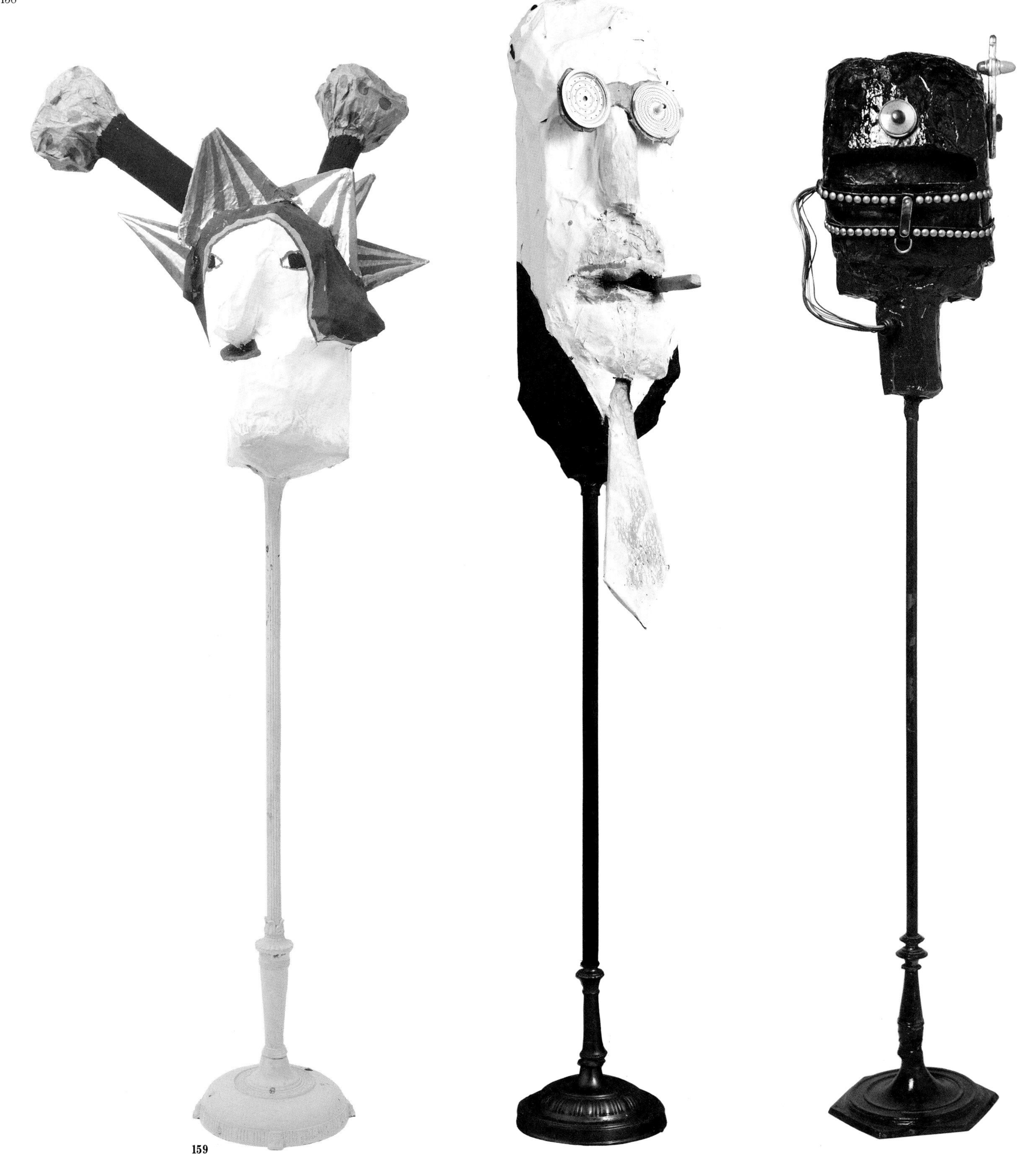

159

[159] I did a series of *papier mâché* sculptures between 1967 and 1971. I had used the material as an illustration tool earlier, but these later figures were for my own amusement. The heads on the left were mounted on floor lamp bases. The double portrait is a bas relief, which I did without any point of reference. Only after it was completed did I realize that it represented a couple from Miami Beach, and that the single head was an unintended caricature of the late Adam Clayton Powell, Harlem's controversial Congressman.

[160] This serigraph was originally done as an illustration for a *Sports Illustrated* essay on the Daytona stock car races. I was sent down to cover the event by the art director, who knew that my interest would not be in the race itself but in the peripheral activity. While the drama was on the track, the real theater—to me—was in the infield where spectators from all over the country congregated. I worked from my own 35mm color photographs.

160

161

[161] Television, a dominant force in our lives, affects us in many ways. Between 1980 and 1983, I worked on a series of 27 acrylic paintings, all 30" x 40," on the subject of television. Since I watch TV while I paint, I was provided with a ready-made model. In this work, I had no hidden agenda or message I wanted to convey, and no client to please. In contrast to my applied work, which is preplanned, I had no idea how the paintings would evolve, but watching the unconscious image emerge through the paint gave me great satisfaction. Illustration is externally generated; painting is an internal process.

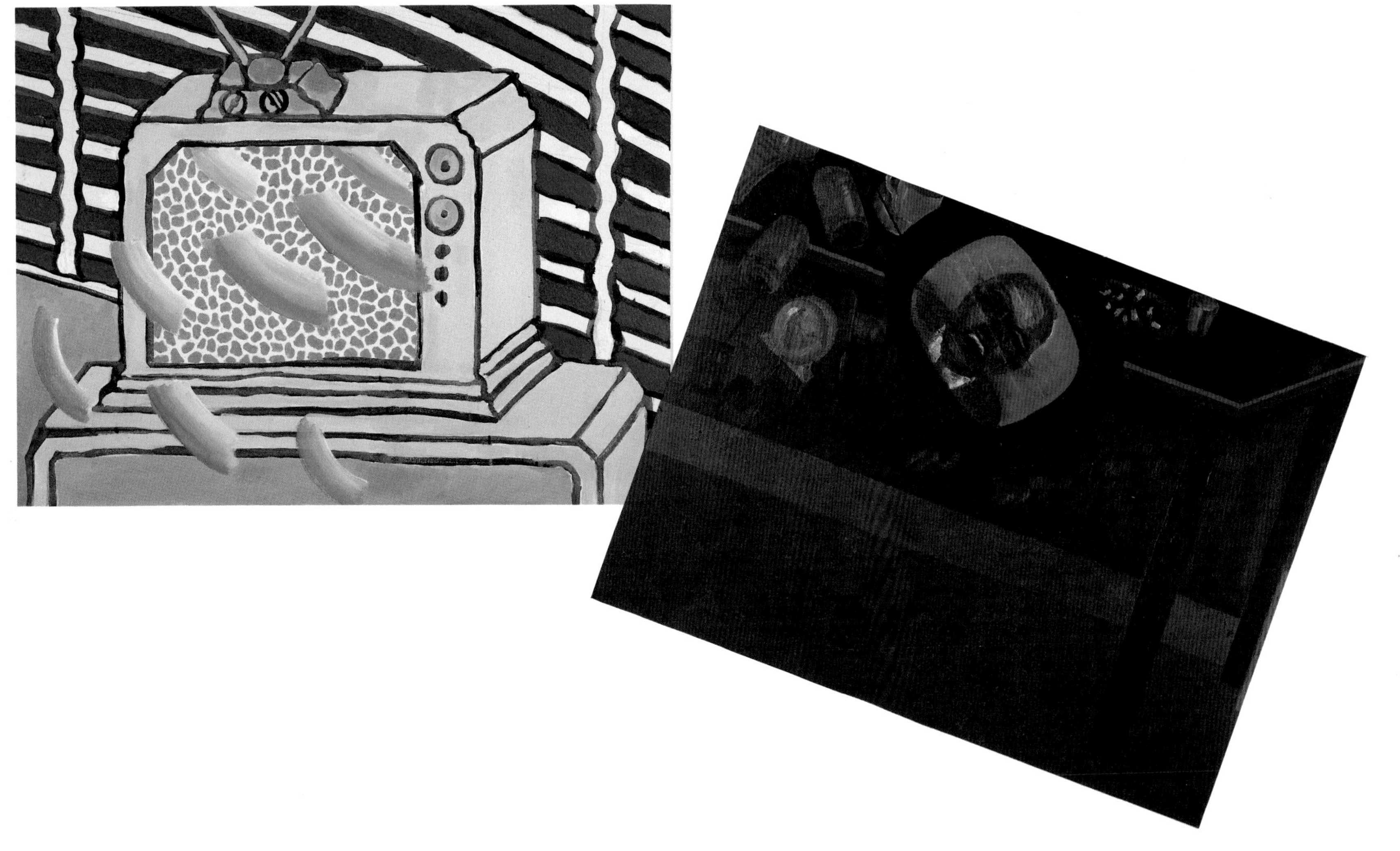